SHANIA TWAIN

OVERCOMING ADVERSITY

SHANIA TWAIN

Dwayne E. Pickels

Introduction by James Scott Brady,
Trustee, the Center to Prevent Handgun Violence
Vice Chairman, the Brain Injury Foundation

Chelsea House Publishers
Philadelphia

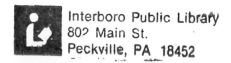

Frontispiece: The acknowledged queen of country music, Shania Twain faced personal challenges and overcame adversity on her way to building a stunning career.

PRODUCED BY 21st Century Publishing and Communications, Inc.

CHELSEA HOUSE PUBLISHERS

EDITOR IN CHIEF Sally Cheney
ASSOCIATE EDITOR IN CHIEF Kim Shinners
PRODUCTION MANAGER Pamela Loos
ART DIRECTOR Sara Davis
COVER DESIGNER tk
COVER PHOTO tk

First Printing

1 3 5 7 9 8 6 4 2

The Chelsea House World Wide Web address is
http://www.chelseahouse.com

Library of Congress Cataloging-in-Publication Data

Pickels, Dwayne E.
Shania Twain / by Dwayne E. Pickels.
    p.   cm. — (Overcoming adversity)
Includes bibliographical references and index.
Summary: Discusses the personal life and professional singing career of the award-winning country music star from Canada, Shania Twain.
ISBN 0-7910-5901-4 — ISBN 0-7910-5902-2 (pb)
1. Twain, Shania—Juvenile literature. 2. Country musicians—Biography—Juvenile literature. [1. Twain, Shania. 2. Singers. 3. Country music—Biography. 4. Women —Biography.] I. Title. II. Series.
ML3930.T88 P53 2000
782.421642'092—dc21
[B]   00-023680

CONTENTS

OVERCOMING ADVERSITY

TIM ALLEN
comedian/performer

MAYA ANGELOU
author

APOLLO 13 MISSION
astronauts

LANCE ARMSTRONG
professional cyclist

DREW BARRYMORE
actress

JAMES BRADY
gun control activist

DREW CAREY
comedian/performer

JIM CARREY
comedian/performer

BILL CLINTON
U.S. president

TOM CRUISE
actor

MICHAEL J. FOX
actor

WHOOPI GOLDBERG
comedian/performer

EKATERINA GORDEEVA
figure skater

SCOTT HAMILTON
figure skater

JEWEL
singer and poet

JAMES EARL JONES
actor

QUINCY JONES
musician and producer

ABRAHAM LINCOLN
U.S. president

WILLIAM PENN
Pennsylvania's founder

JACKIE ROBINSON
baseball legend

ROSEANNE
entertainer

MONICA SELES
tennis star

SAMMY SOSA
baseball star

DAVE THOMAS
entrepreneur

SHANIA TWAIN
entertainer

ROBIN WILLIAMS
performer

STEVIE WONDER
entertainer

ON FACING ADVERSITY

James Scott Brady

I GUESS IT'S a long way from a Centralia, Illinois, train yard to the George Washington University Hospital Trauma Unit. My dad was a yardmaster for the old Chicago, Burlington & Quincy Railroad. As a child, I used to get to sit in the engineer's lap and imagine what it was like to drive that train. I guess I always have liked being in the "driver's seat."

Years later, however, my interest turned from driving trains to driving campaigns. In 1979, former Texas governor John Connally hired me as a press secretary in his campaign for the American presidency. We lost the Republican primary to a former Hollywood star named Ronald Reagan. But I managed to jump over to the Reagan campaign. When Reagan was elected in 1980, I was "sitting in the catbird seat," as humorist James Thurber would say—poised to be named presidential press secretary. I held that title throughout the eight years of the Reagan administration. But not without one terrible, extended interruption.

It happened barely two months after the Reagan administration took office. I never even heard the shots. On March 30, 1981, my life went blank in an instant. In an attempt to assassinate President Reagan, John Hinckley Jr. armed himself with a "Saturday night special"—a low-quality, $29 pistol—and shot wildly as our presidential entourage exited a Washington hotel. One of the exploding bullets struck me just above the left eye. It shattered into a couple dozen fragments, some of which penetrated my skull and entered my brain.

The next few months of my life were a nightmare of repeated surgery, broken contact with the outside world, and a variety of medical complications. More than once, I was very close to death.

The next few years were filled with frustrating struggles to function with a paralyzed right side, struggles to speak and communicate.

To people who face and defeat daunting obstacles, "ambition" is not becoming wealthy or famous or winning elections or awards. Words like "ambition" and "achievement" and "success" take on very different meanings. The objective is just to live, to wake up every morning. The goals are not lofty; they are very ordinary.

My own heroes are ordinary folks—but they accomplish extraordinary things because they try. My greatest hero is my wife, Sarah. She's accomplished a lot of things in life, but two stand out. The first has been the way she has cared for me and our son since I was shot. A tremendous tragedy and burden was dropped unexpectedly into her life, totally beyond her control and without justification. She could have given up; instead, she focused her energies on preserving our family and returning our lives to normal as much as possible. Week by week, month by month, year by year, she has not reached for the miraculous, just for the normal. Yet in focusing on the normal, she has helped accomplish the miraculous.

Her other most remarkable accomplishment, to me, has been spearheading the effort to keep guns out of the hands of criminals and children in America. Opponents call her a "gun grabber"; I call her a national hero. And I am not alone.

After a seven-year battle, during which Sarah and I worked tirelessly to educate the public about the need for stronger gun laws, the Brady Bill became law in 1993. It was a victory, achieved in the face of tremendous opposition, that now benefits all Americans. From the time the law took effect through fall 1997, background checks had stopped 173,000 criminals and other high-risk purchasers from buying handguns, and the law has helped to reduce illegal gun trafficking.

Sarah was not pursuing fame, or even recognition. She simply started at one point—when our son, Scott, found a loaded handgun on the seat of a pickup truck and, thinking it was a toy, pointed it at Sarah.

Fortunately, no one was hurt. But seeing a gun nearly bring a second tragedy upon our family, Sarah became determined to do whatever she could to prevent senseless death and injury from guns.

Some people think of Sarah as a powerful political force. To me, she's the person who so many times fed me and helped me dress during my long years of recovery.

Overcoming obstacles is part of life, not just for people who are challenged by disabilities, illnesses, or tragedies, but for all people. No matter what the obstacle—fear, disability, prejudice, grief, or a difficulty that isn't likely to "just go away"—we can all work to make this world a better place.

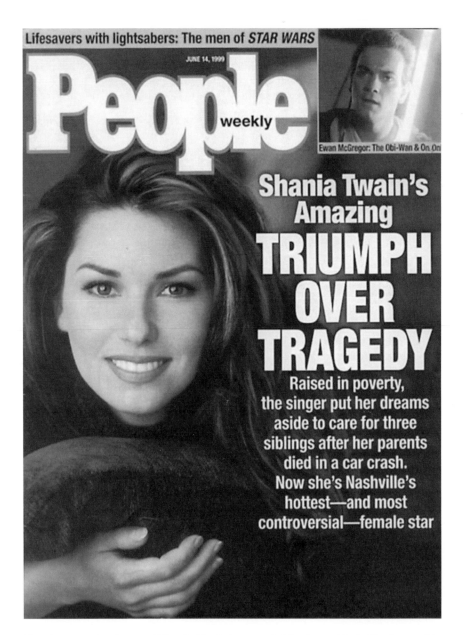

People *magazine honored Shania Twain's remarkable rise to Nashville fame with a glowing cover in 1999. In only a few short years, the young singer from Canada made her way from near obscurity to become country music's hottest superstar.*

1

ON HER WAY

NOVEMBER 1, 1987, was a wintry day in the province of Ontario, Canada. In Ontario's capital city, Toronto, the telephone rang in the home of Eilleen Regina Twain. The young singer felt an inexplicable sense of dread as a friend picked up the phone. "After my friend took the call first, I knew right away that something was very wrong and my heart was just jumping out of my chest. . . . I was freaking before I even got on the phone," she recalled.

Eilleen took the phone. The strained voice at the other end of the line belonged to her older sister, Jill, who broke the terrible news: their parents, Sharon and Jerry Twain, had been killed when their car was hit head-on by a logging truck on an Ontario highway. Their young brother Mark, who was with their parents, survived with minor injuries. The news changed Eilleen's life in an instant.

Jill was married with a family of her own, but sister Carrie-Ann and brothers Mark and Darryl were teenagers and now orphans who had to be cared for. A devastated Eilleen knew what she had to do.

She packed her belongings, quit her job, and returned to her hometown of Timmins, Ontario, to take responsibility for her three younger siblings.

Eilleen later confessed that it was a distressing time for her and that she was often scared and insecure. "I was overwhelmed with a lot of decisions," she said, but she added that "what I learned through all of that was how strong I was capable of being. I didn't fall apart. . . ."

Eilleen faced the challenge of looking after her sister and brothers with the same dedication and determination that had driven her to pursue a music career. The 22-year-old woman had overcome many obstacles to get to Toronto and that fateful phone call.

Growing up in Timmins, Eilleen had always seemed to know that music was going to be her life. Her musical talent was obvious. As a child she loved to listen to the radio and sing along to the music. From an early age, encouraged by her parents, she sang and played guitar in local clubs around her hometown. In her teens Eilleen was a celebrity around Timmins. She appeared on radio and television, sang at senior centers, and performed at community gatherings and fairs.

But Eilleen yearned for more than small-town life and local performances. She needed to leave the security of home and family to fulfill her ambitions. At 21, with her parents' blessing, Eilleen packed her bags and headed for Canada's show business capital, Toronto. With a day job as a secretary, she entertained in clubs at night and dreamed of a career as a country singer.

That dream appeared to be shattered when tragedy struck with the death of her parents. As a devastated Eilleen hurried home to take on the responsibility of a family, she could not know what the future would be.

Eilleen would have been stunned if she had known that in little more than a decade, with only three albums behind her, she would reign as the top-selling female

country music artist. Eilleen's phenomenal career has brought her Grammy Awards and scores of other accolades and honors. From an often impoverished youth, she has fulfilled her dream of financial independence. Along the way, she married a successful record producer and songwriter, Robert "Mutt" Lange, who encouraged her to revolutionize her music.

Eilleen has toured and performed at sold-out, mega-event concerts, often amid a blaze of brilliant fireworks

By 1999, with only three albums to her credit, Shania was touring and performing to sold-out audiences. In concert in Devone, California, she displays the unique musical style that has won her fame and fortune.

Scores of honors have been showered on Shania. Here she poses with one of the music industry's most prestigious awards, Entertainer of the Year from the Country Music Association. In 1999, Shania was the first woman to win the award in 13 years.

and surrounded by some of the world's finest musicians. She has traveled to exotic places, such as Egypt, to film her music videos. Her image has appeared in countless magazines as Revlon cosmetics tapped her for its ad campaigns. A fitness magazine for men named her one of the 10 sexiest women on the planet. For U.S. troops overseas, she topped the list of entertainers they most wanted to see and hear. Millions of fans enthuse over this 5'4", green-eyed brunette whose innovative style has made her a giant in the music world.

Eilleen Regina Twain is a household name, but not as "Eilleen." The world knows her as "Shania," the name she chose in 1991 as she rose to fame. To honor her Native American heritage, she took her new name from an Ojibwa Indian word that means "I'm on my way." In the new millennium, Shania Twain is indeed on her way.

At age 18, when she posed for this promotion photo, Shania was still known as Eilleen Regina Twain. From childhood she had sung and played guitar on the northern Ontario club circuit. But young Eilleen had higher ambitions, which a family tragedy nearly destroyed.

2

"LIKE A FEATHER IN THE WIND . . ."

BEFORE ANY FUTURE triumphs could be won, however, Eilleen needed to face the present. In Timmins, she settled her parents' affairs, selling their business, buying a truck, and settling down to take on her new responsibilities. It seemed as if she had abandoned her music to raise and care for her young, struggling family. She recalled that at the time, she "didn't see music fitting in. In order to fix [these] broken things, there was no time for music," she said.

Remembering her emotions at the time, the singer also later confided to an interviewer, "Yes, you can lose somebody overnight. Yes, your whole life can be turned upside down. Life is short. It can come and go like a feather in the wind." Despite her grieving and her loss, Eilleen's priority was her remaining family.

Eilleen's devotion to family reflected the world in which she was born and grew up. Family was the most important thing, and relationships meant more than career success. Although Timmins is Eilleen's hometown, she was born in Windsor, Ontario, on August 28, 1965. She

17

was the second daughter of Clarence and Sharon Edwards. Her older sister was Jill, and when Eilleen was a toddler, another sister, Carrie-Ann, joined the family. The girls' parents were growing apart, however, and they separated and divorced.

Sharon moved to Timmins, a gold-mining town 500 miles north of Toronto, with her three little girls. There, Sharon met and married Gerald "Jerry" Twain. An Ojibwa Indian, Jerry Twain struggled to make a living working as a gold prospector and forester. Two boys, Mark and Daryl, were soon added to the family. Although the boys were the girls' half-brothers, Jerry and Sharon did not use that word. They were all brothers and sisters. "We were all just family," Eilleen later explained.

Eilleen has always considered Jerry her real father. And she was delighted when he adopted her and her sisters. Jerry also persuaded the Ojibwa tribe, called the First Nation, to give the three sisters membership in the tribe. When Eilleen took her Ojibwa name "Shania," she didn't reveal at the time that Jerry had been her stepfather. In 1996, a newspaper in Timmins dug up the story and exposed the singer's deception, accusing her of exploiting her so-called Native American heritage for publicity purposes. Eilleen has explained simply, "My dad's side of the family was the side we grew up with. So it was the Indians that were really our family."

Many of Eilleen's fondest memories are of her child-hood visits to her Ojibwa grandparents. Jerry's mother and father and other members of the tribe took Eilleen hunting and camping and taught her Native American ways. The little girl learned important lessons from them about nature and the environment.

Eilleen's family faced many hardships during her child-hood. Jerry tried hard to scratch out a living as a miner and forester. The family often moved from town to town as Jerry looked for better opportunities. Sharon stayed at home and looked after their children. Sometimes living on

the brink of poverty, Eilleen remembers going hunting with Jerry for rabbits and even moose to supplement the family's meager food supply. There were times when all the family had to eat was bread, milk, and sugar. When she went to school, she often toted mustard sandwiches and identified better-off students as coming from "roast beef" families. But the little girl did not complain about her family's difficulties. In fact, she tried to hide them from teachers and schoolmates. She was afraid that authorities might probe into her family's plight and take her away from the people she loved.

One thing Eilleen could not conceal was her passion for music. As a toddler, she loved to hide away in her bedroom and hum and sing tunes like "Twinkle, Twinkle, Little Star." When Sharon heard the little girl, she realized her

A gold-mining facility rises above the town of Timmins in northern Ontario. Growing up in Timmins, Eilleen and her family were often poor. But hard times did not deter the determined young woman from her goals of a singing career.

daughter had musical talent. According to Eilleen, she made her unofficial singing debut when she was only three. She was in a restaurant singing along with the jukebox when her mother lifted her onto a countertop and urged her to sing for the customers.

Eilleen's second public performance was in the first grade. She did a show-and-tell stint for her classmates, delivering a rousing rendition of John Denver's "Take Me Home, Country Roads." She later confessed that she was less than a hit with her fellow students. Their childish ribbing and teasing made the little girl feel self-conscious. Apparently some even made fun of her name, calling her "Twang." Eilleen's feelings were deeply hurt, and she later recalled, "It really created serious inhibitions for me. From that point on, I was afraid to perform."

Eilleen gradually overcame her insecurities through the support of her parents. Sharon and Jerry continued to prod her toward a musical career. By the time she was in the eighth grade, Eilleen was playing the guitar, a gift from her parents. Jerry taught her to play some chords, and soon she was strumming her first songs—country tunes. It was natural that Eilleen would be drawn to country music. Her parents were avid fans, and she grew up listening to the stars of country music. The radio was on most of the time and tuned to stations that played singers like Dolly Parton, Tammy Wynette, and Willie Nelson. The family also enjoyed the sounds of groups like the Mamas and the Papas, the Carpenters, and Eilleen's favorite, Stevie Wonder.

Eilleen soon graduated from playing at home to playing and singing with her Indian cousins in a band that entertained at family gatherings. From that humble beginning, the young singer branched out to sing at local clubs, community gatherings, fairs and festivals, talent contests—even on local television. She was becoming a celebrity around Timmins.

Sharon Twain was the prime mover behind her young daughter's budding musical career, which also included writing some of her own songs. Sharon dressed Eilleen in

As a child, Eilleen was an avid music fan, spending long hours tuning in the radio to country and pop music. Her favorite entertainer was Stevie Wonder, a popular young singer and pianist in the 1960s and 1970s.

stage outfits sewn by Jerry's mother and tried to persuade local bands to book the girl as a singer. Eilleen has recalled that her parents sometimes dragged her out of bed at one in the morning to appear with a band. The hour was so late because Canadian law didn't allow minors in clubs until they stopped selling liquor, which was at 1 A.M. Eilleen remembers that she would "get up and sing a few songs with the band and before I knew it, I was actually doing clubs professionally." She also confided to an interviewer that "I pretty much missed my childhood. I've always been focused. My career has always been very consuming."

When Eilleen was 12 years old, she met Mary Bailey, a woman who would play an important role in the young singer's musical career. Eilleen was singing at a concert in Sudbury, Ontario, where Bailey was the headline performer. After hearing the preteen sing Hank Williams's "I'm So Lonesome I Could Cry," Bailey introduced herself to Sharon and told her how impressed she was with the girl's voice.

Mary Bailey, a country music singer, had toured the country circuit for several years. Like Eilleen, Mary had begun singing when she was a child of five. Unlike Eilleen, however, Bailey had given up singing when she was 12. She wanted to have a normal adolescence. When Bailey began her career again in her twenties, she was preparing to release her first album, *Mystery Lady*, for RCA records. Bailey kept in touch with Eilleen and her family for the next several years.

Eilleen's career got a big boost in 1978 when the teenager performed on a popular Canadian television show. *The Tommy Hunter Show*, a variety showcase for hopeful country singers like Eilleen, also featured established singers like the popular Glen Campbell. To appear on this show was a major step to a country music career for a young singer. Eilleen also made guest appearances on the popular Canadian television shows *Opry North* and *Easy Country*.

Getting to and from musical gigs was not always easy. Sometimes Eilleen had to travel by herself when money was short. It was on one of these trips for a television appearance that she displayed her determination and independence. Boarding a train for the 500-mile journey to Toronto, she discovered about an hour into the trip that she was on the wrong train. Confronting the conductor, she insisted he stop the train and let her off. "I'm going to be on TV tomorrow night. I have to be there. I gotta get off this train," she implored.

Apparently impressed with this teenager's spunk, the conductor complied, and Eilleen got off along the deserted railroad tracks with just her guitar. For an hour, while she strummed her music, she waited for the right train to roll by and carry her to her performance. Recalling the incident, she laughed, "It was just so funny. I remember thinking at the time, 'This is a song.'" Even at a young age, Eilleen was thinking of how to put her experiences into her music.

Shania once confessed to an interviewer that as a child she didn't have ambitions as a singer. "I didn't think that I would grow up to be a singer," she explained. "I was already a singer." As a teenager, music and singing were a large part of her life, but not all of it. She studied at the Timmins high school and enjoyed athletics. Her games were basketball and volleyball, and she was a member of the school's gymnastics team. She has said that she also spent a lot of time by herself writing songs. Eilleen also played the tomboy. She later confided that as her figure developed, she tried to hide her womanly curves because she didn't want to stand out. She would often put on layers of clothes and flatten out her chest. She was trying to avoid the attentions of boys just because she had a shapely figure.

Family activities were also a large part of Eilleen's growing up. She loved to be outdoors, camping and hiking and learning outdoor skills from her Ojibwa father and grandparents. The family roughed it in the woods, pitching a tent or sleeping in the back of their truck.

Her love of the outdoors and her athletic abilities came in handy when she began working with her father while she was in high school. Jerry had scraped together enough money to start a tree-planting business, and Eilleen was delighted to be part of it. For several summers, she lived in a camp in the woods from which her father ran the operations. The business was a family affair. Sharon looked after the camp, Eilleen's grandparents ran the camp kitchen, and her aunt back in Timmins did the bookkeeping. Eilleen became the foreman of a crew that planted the trees. She later described those days of hard work and the inconveniences, including bathing in the lake and never using shampoo because it would attract insects. "It was a simple way of living, and I loved it." She also added, "And I miss it."

Eilleen learned the guitar as a child and often provided her own accompaniment when she toured the clubs. As a teenager, she was turning toward rock music and was undecided about choosing between country or rock.

Music, however, was Eilleen's first love. On weekends, while still in high school, she played the music circuit around northern Ontario. At 16 she joined a band called Longshot, whose leader had been impressed with her voice when he saw her on television. Longshot was a popular band at clubs and parties around Timmins. But it was essentially a rock group, and Eilleen was known as a country singer. Sharon and Jerry were concerned that their daughter would turn from their beloved country to rock. When Longshot split up, Eilleen continued touring the Ontario circuit with other rock bands. Often, the bands opened the shows for well-known groups that toured Ontario. At this point, however, Eilleen was ambivalent about her music. Would it be rock or country?

For a time, Eilleen chose rock. After graduating from high school, she continued appearing with rock bands in the clubs and bars around Timmins. The scene could often be rowdy when customers drank too much, but Eilleen has said it didn't bother her. "There's something more moving about music than anything else in life for me," she later said. "It's like a drug. I spent my teen years being high on music."

It wasn't only music that kept Eilleen from the drug and alcohol scene. Jerry taught her a lesson about the damage alcohol can do when Eilleen was only 13. It was holiday time, and her parents were celebrating with a few drinks. According to Eilleen, Jerry and Sharon seldom drank and never had liquor in the house. Curious about what a drink tasted like, she asked for a sip. Jerry gave Eilleen a little and then some more until Eilleen was getting drunk. When she tried to sing and play her guitar, she slurred her words. Her parents piled her into bed and waited for the liquor to wear off. As Eilleen recalls, she felt awful the next day. From that time on, alcohol was never a temptation for her.

Eilleen seemed content to play and sing in clubs across northern Ontario. But her music was attracting attention, and at 17 she signed a contract with an erstwhile manager and tried out in Nashville, Tennessee. Nashville, the capital of country music, wasn't yet ready for the young singer, and Eilleen returned to Timmins without any deals.

Wondering how she could further her daughter's career, Sharon Twain got in touch with Mary Bailey. Bailey agreed to be Eilleen's manager and show her the ropes of the country music business. One of Bailey's first moves was to take Eilleen to Nashville again. Nothing came of the second trip either. Nashville wasn't much interested then in teenage singers. And Eilleen still seemed more interested in rock and pop music. She and Mary Bailey ended their business relationship.

Eilleen was not totally finished with country music, however. In 1984, the Canadian magazine *Country Music News* published an article about record producer and disc jockey Stan Campbell, who was based in Toronto. Along with her picture, Eilleen got more than a mention when Campbell praised her singing and her potential in the article. "Eilleen possesses a powerful voice with an impressive range," Campbell said, adding that "she has the necessary drive, ambition, and positive attitude to achieve her goals."

With this boost to her career came another opportunity when Campbell was preparing a record project for a Canadian singer named Tim Denis. Campbell asked Eilleen to be the backup singer and cut a duet with Denis. The song, "Heavy on the Sunshine," appeared on Denis's debut album, released in 1985. That same year, Eilleen got another backup spot when producer Tony Migliore was cutting an album for Kelita Haverland, a Canadian singer. Migliore asked Eilleen to do backup vocals for Haverland. The album did score a hit, but backup vocals were not going to carry Eilleen to recording contracts and stardom.

Eilleen finally made a gut-wrenching decision. She knew she had to break free of her image as a small-town singer. The place to begin a national recording career was Toronto, a cosmopolitan city that presented more music opportunities. Singing in the evenings and on weekends, she appeared with a variety of bands, performing a variety of singing styles and interpreting other singers' music. A highlight of her Toronto stint was when she opened a show for Broadway musical star Bernadette Peters, who was performing with the Toronto Symphony. Eilleen was determined to reach her goal and was sure she could make it when the tragedy of her parents' sudden deaths struck.

Back in Timmins, Eilleen felt the full weight of her new responsibilities. Carrie-Ann was 18 and pretty much able to take care of herself, but the boys, Mark and Darryl, were young teens.

"It was like being thrown into the deep end of a pool and just having to swim," Shania recalled. The young woman was scared and feeling desperate. But her strength and her

ability to put things in perspective gave her the courage to face whatever was to come.

For a time, it looked as if Eilleen would be facing the poverty she had so often known growing up. "I was so numb," she said. "Nothing penetrated. It was a very difficult time. But, boy, oh boy, did I ever get strong." Eilleen's extended family could only give so much help, and she needed a permanent job. In her search for some stability, Eilleen called on her old friend and mentor, Mary Bailey, who encouraged her not to give up her music dreams. Bailey arranged some auditions for Eilleen, but most importantly, she advised her to get a steady gig with a regular paycheck. Calling on Bailey for help and following her advice put Eilleen on the path to fulfilling her dreams.

With its many theaters and music venues, Toronto was the place for an aspiring young singer to get a start. Working in the day and singing in clubs at night, Eilleen had some success until her ambitions were cut short by her parents' untimely deaths.

Eilleen's infectious smile and onstage charm were tremendous assets as she struggled to be noticed in the music world. Finding her own identity as a singer took grit and determination as she rose from singing in an Ontario resort to her breakthrough as a recording artist in Nashville, Tennessee.

3

FINDING AN IDENTITY

MARY BAILEY POURED her energies into finding a spot for Eilleen. She struck gold when, in 1988, a resort hotel about 150 miles north of Toronto booked the 23-year-old singer for its nightclub act.

The resort, Deerhurst, was near Huntsville, Ontario, and was a favorite place for tourists and vacationers from Toronto. Eilleen would not have to depend on touring and she would have a reliable income. Packing up once more, the young woman moved her family to Huntsville.

Deerhurst was a far cry from the smoky bars and clubs of northern Ontario. The resort featured dinner theater and a dance review called Viva Vegas. Since Deerhurst didn't cater to the same audience on a regular basis, tourists and vacationers came and went. For Eilleen, this presented the chance to work with a different audience each night. She had to display all her considerable talents to win their attention and applause. She had to entertain while she sang. Deerhurst also introduced Eilleen to a variety of styles of music, from

Motown to Gershwin and from country to pop. Eilleen sang all the styles. She also met professionals in the business and learned from them.

It was while Eilleen was at Deerhurst that she first heard the name "Shania." In talking with a young wardrobe assistant backstage, Eilleen asked the woman, whose name was Shania, what it meant. When the assistant explained that it was an Ojibwa name meaning "I'm on my way," Eilleen replied, "You know, my dad was Ojibwa."

In speaking of her experience at Deerhurst, Eilleen has explained how it influenced her stage presence: "First, I was able to overcome a lot of the inhibitions I had left about performing. It's easy to get up and sing in a country bar, where it's just a party, but when you're in front of a lot of people and you're essentially on a pedestal and everyone stops to listen, you've got to start *performing*." Eilleen also learned a great deal about theatrical staging, choreography, and production. "I got a really good taste of what I'm doing now," she explained.

At the same time, Eilleen took care of her brothers. She drove them back and forth to school, dances, and games. She went to parent-teacher meetings at school. Mark later recalled that his sister was very strict. She was going to keep them on the right path.

Eilleen performed at Deerhurst for three years, during which time the boys graduated from high school and finally moved away on their own. She was torn between sadness at their leaving and a certain elation that at last she was responsible only for herself. As she later put it, "It was like, 'I'm free!' I said, 'Now what am I gonna do with my new life?' I decided I wanted to go for it!"

Going for it meant getting to the right people, and that was part of Mary Bailey's job. During the years at Deerhurst, Eilleen and Mary had formed a strong bond that was more like mother and daughter than manager and client. Mary loved the young woman whose talent she had admired so early on and had encouraged and promoted.

She was tireless in working to have her aspiring young client noticed. She poured time and money into transforming Eilleen into a glamorous professional who would take the music industry by storm. To showcase the young singer, Mary invested her personal resources in stage costumes, sound equipment, musicians, and first-class traveling. No more pickup trucks for Eilleen.

To step up Eilleen's career, it was essential that influential people in the business hear her music. Through contacts, Mary sent a tape with some of Eilleen's music to a man named Dick Frank in Nashville. Frank was a well-connected entertainment attorney who had represented such industry giants as the Everly Brothers and Patsy Cline. He was also one of the founders of the Country Music Association (CMA), the prestigious organization whose awards and honors are highly coveted by country stars. Eilleen knew that Nashville was the place to be if one wanted to be a country music star. Despite her unfortunate early experiences in Nashville, Eilleen was excited at the prospect of a possible introduction to the Nashville scene.

Frank was impressed with Eilleen's voice, but it was important that he see her perform live. The attorney journeyed to Deerhurst, and as he sat in the audience that night, he immediately recognized Eilleen's natural talent. Obviously enthralled with Eilleen's strong voice and stage presence, Frank got in touch with a Nashville colleague, Norro Wilson. A songwriter, producer, and mover and shaker in Nashville, Wilson wrote the Charlie Rich hit "The Most Beautiful Girl in the World" and had produced records for such classic and contemporary country stars as George Jones, Tammy Wynette, and Sammy Kershaw. Wilson listened to Eilleen's tape and agreed to give her a chance to make a demo tape in Nashville.

With high hopes, Eilleen and Mary Bailey flew to Nashville and met Norro Wilson. Not long after their initial meeting, Wilson invited Eilleen to a studio to start

Nashville, Tennessee, is the capital of country music and the place for a young country singer to launch a career. When record producers heard Eilleen, they were so impressed they handed her a multirecord deal, almost unheard of for a relative unknown.

recording. Somewhat daunted by her first experience with a professional music production, and knowing the importance of impressing Nashville's music elite, Eilleen was apprehensive. Sensing her nervousness, Wilson went out of his way to put her at ease. His folksy manner was soothing. "Just want to get some things down on tape here," he said. "I already know you're good. I can hear that. I want to try a few things with you, see what suits you best."

Once Eilleen began to sing, there was little question that she was going to make it. According to Dick Frank, who was in the studio, "You could've heard a pin drop as soon as she hit her first note. After what I had heard, I had no doubt we could get a recording contract for her."

Getting the contract, however, required involving other industry giants. With three songs on tape, Wilson passed Eilleen on to Buddy Cannon, an executive with Mercury Records. A delighted Cannon passed on his recommendation to Harold Shedd, head of Mercury's Nashville division. Shedd is credited with discovering some of modern country music's hottest entertainers, including the band Alabama and singers Billy Ray Cyrus, Sammy Kershaw, Terri Clark, and Toby Keith. It was Shedd who inked Eilleen's deal with Mercury, after agreeing to work with Norro Wilson to produce the singer's debut album.

First, Eilleen had to have a stage name. Shedd didn't like the sound of her name. He thought "Eilleen" didn't fit well with "Twain." According to the singer, they wanted to change her last name, but she balked, unwilling to let go of her identity as a Twain. She preferred to change her first name. Remembering the young woman at Deerhurst, Eilleen Twain became Shania Twain. As she recalls, "I thought, wow, it's Indian, and it flows so well with Twain."

With a new name and a multirecord deal in tow, Shania Twain was slated to begin recording with Wilson and Shedd just as soon as Shedd wrapped up production of an album by another hot young newcomer, Billy Ray Cyrus. That project, called *Some Gave All*, contained the smash crossover hit "Achy Breaky Heart." Shedd and his colleagues at Mercury were itching to repeat the quakes that song sent rumbling through the charts.

Publicists and image consultants set upon Shania to promote her image, and major-league songwriters were rounded up to provide the material to launch her on her way. No one thought to ask Shania if she could write music, or even if she wanted to. And at that precarious point in her career, she didn't feel she was in a position to assert herself. It was better, she concluded, to let pros

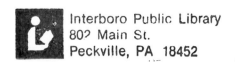

handle her debut and just worry about doing what was expected of her, at least for the time being.

Shania knew she was going into the studio with some of the best session players in the business. Larrie Londin would be on drums, with Reggie Young on guitar, Glen Worf on bass, Billy Joe Walker on acoustic guitar, and Sonny Garrish on steel guitar. Collectively, these powerhouse musicians had played with some of the premier names in country and pop music. They had backed performers like Johnny Cash, Waylon Jennings, Elvis Presley, Chet Atkins, the Everly Brothers, Jimmy Buffett, and Mark Knopfler of Dire Straits.

Other illustrious musicians were also included in Shania's backup band. On electric guitar was Steve Gibson, with Chris Leuzinger on acoustic guitar, and Allen Frank Estes, Mark Casstevens, and John Willis on rhythm guitar. Mike Brignardello was on bass, Paul Leim on drums, and David Briggs, Gary Prim, and Costo Davis on keyboards. Additional synthesizer duties were handled by Davis, with Jelly Roll Johnson and Terry McMillan pitching in for harmonica and additional percussion chores. Anthony Martin, Ronny Scaife, John Wesley Ryles, Cindy Walker, Dennis Wilson, and Curtis Young provided background vocals. In the few short months since she had met Dick Frank, Shania was being showered with talent to accompany her maiden recording effort.

Although the album was titled *Shania Twain*, the singer still felt something was missing. She was right. In the liner notes her name appeared only once, as cowriter beside Kent Robbins under a single song title, "God Ain't Gonna Getcha for That." The song tells of a young woman in a rowdy bar who approaches a man sitting all by himself. He hasn't joined in the singing and dancing, and she offers to buy him a beer. She tells him to lighten up and have fun, remarking, "God ain't gonna getcha for that." It was the kind of theme Shania would express later when she was free to write her own music.

Eilleen was not always pleased with her early recording experiences in Nashville, feeling her songwriting talents were not recognized. By 1999, when Eilleen, now Shania, was rehearsing at Nashville's famed Grand Ole Opry house, her artistry as singer and songwriter were known throughout the country.

Of the 10 songs, "God Ain't Gonna Getcha for That" was the only one she had a hand in writing. Robbins, who had penned a number of hit songs for, among others, the Judds and Ronnie Milsap, was one of the many songwriters contracted for the recording. And he had another cowritten number on the album. Shania was confused and disappointed. She knew she could write great songs, and she wanted to sing them and sound like herself, not just some country singer belting out someone else's music.

Shania vented her feelings about the Nashville song mill and how it differed from the way she had tapped her creative spirit from the time she was a child. "People write together like they are going to lunch together. They make appointments. So this was very new to me, and I was kind of intimidated by it."

Norro Wilson understood her frustration. He explained that formula or not, it was simply the way the music was produced. It was a kind of dictatorship, he admitted, but there was usually a dictatorship with a start-up artist. In a later interview, Wilson explained how it worked with Shania. "We would state to her that, if her song that she wrote, or songs, held up in comparison to the other songs that we had chosen, that would be fine. We would do that. Our committee of people at the time, we didn't care where it came from, as long as we had a hit or two."

For the sake of a future career, Shania did what she had to do. Her lack of personal input began to eat at her, however. "I didn't want my recording career to be that," she has said. "I didn't want my recording to be cover material, I didn't want it to be 9-5 songwriting and controlled by everybody else."

Shania has maintained that she is first and foremost a singer-songwriter. Even as a child, she found more solace in retiring to the privacy and security of her room to write songs than in performing other people's material. To omit that aspect of herself from the product was something like recording in mono rather than stereo.

Shedd and Wilson assured Shania that her songs were fine. They warned, however, that country music radio stations did not take well to anything that was different from what they played. Tradition, they explained, ruled the airwaves, and her writing was not traditional enough. They insisted that the formula formats of the songs they selected for her were more likely to score country airtime and a place on the charts. Shania could, she was told, exert more of her own influence once she had built a fan base.

Aside from her voice, of course, Shania's input in the creation of songs was obviously minimal. Despite her feelings of uneasiness, however, she was grateful. In 1993, when her debut album, *Shania Twain*, was released, she used her liner notes to thank Dick Frank "For believing in me enough to get the whole thing started and for going that extra mile." She also thanked the numerous people who had recorded and mixed the album as well as "all the wonderful singers and musicians that blessed this album with their talent." Shedd, Wilson, and Buddy Cannon also received her praise. Mary Bailey was honored as being Shania's true friend, and she penned dedications to her family for their years of sacrifice to make her dreams a reality.

Mercury went all out to market and promote the album. The company sent out a three-page biography of the singer to radio shows, booking agents, and the press. The biography described her background in Canada working in the woods and singing in what it chose to call "glamorous resorts and nightspots." Her Native American heritage and her parents' encouragement and sacrifices were stressed. In the bio itself, Shania had this to say: "The funny thing is when I'm in the music world, people can't believe I've ever lived such a rustic life. And people from back home for the most part don't know about the other life I've had. I've never talked about it. They're going to be really shocked when they see this album."

One of Shania's biographers finds this claim not quite

accurate. From her childhood she was a performer and a celebrity in northern Ontario. The folks in Timmins and around the countryside knew her music and her ambitions. What would surprise them was her new name.

In addition to the biography, Mercury put together an itinerary for a concert tour. The company also released a single from the album, "What Made You Say That?" along with a sexy video of Shania romping on a beach in Miami. The video contradicted the image on the album's cover, which tried to exploit her northern beginnings. She is shown in a fur-lined suede coat and boots against piles of snow with a wolf by her side. It must have been confusing for people. But the video did reflect what would become Shania's signature image—a bare midriff.

Despite the impressive production and the people involved, *Shania Twain* was a disappointment. The album sold less than 100,000 copies. Critics were less than enthusiastic, some calling the songs "tepid" and "pedestrian." Shania, however, was singled out for her voice. The *All Music Guide to Country* thought the recording showed Shania's vocal skills but that the songs lacked "strong melodies" and were "mediocre." The guide's critic did, however, write that the album was "a promising debut, largely because it showcases her [Shania's] fine vocal talent." If Shania needed any encouragement to write her own music, the album's reception was a tremendous impetus to become independent.

Shania is fond of saying that her mother always knew her daughter would be a star in the music world. The young singer did make it once she established her own identity. Although she was versatile enough to tackle a variety of music forms, she made her way in country music. "I consider myself a country artist," she told an interviewer. "That music was always such a big part of me growing up. I loved Stevie Wonder and the Carpenters, but Willie Nelson and Dolly Parton were just as big an influence. . . . You've got to fit somewhere, and for the sake of

Although Shania received good reviews for her vocal talents, her first album was not a hit. Still, she was a recognized country music artist, as evidenced by this May 1993 issue of Canada's Country Music News.

fitting, I'm country. I've got no complaints about that. The challenge is to go beyond that."

Although the country music market is more attuned to singles, Shania's "What Made You Say That?" never reached higher than 55 on the country singles chart, landing minimal airtime. The album itself peaked at number 68 on *Billboard*'s Top Country Albums chart in August of 1993. The video too was a disappointment. She didn't get any airtime from that effort. She was, however, noticed in another realm of popular culture.

Shania had always been a fan and admirer of country music's Dolly Parton, shown here with another country star, Vince Gill. Shania credits Parton's artistry as being a major influence on her own musical style.

One of the first to fall for her was moody actor Sean Penn, who had recently been divorced from another famous singer known for baring more than her midriff—Madonna. Penn, a popular film star who was beginning to try his hand behind the camera, wanted to direct a video with Shania based on her album single "Dance with the One That Brought You."

Shania was excited and thrilled to work with Penn, and

the shoot got under way in May 1993. The video starred veteran character actor Charles Durning and took place in a country setting—a barn dance. The story revolves around a guy, Durning, who likes to cut loose at dances with the girls. But his true love, Shania, knows he's just fooling around and that she is the only one. Despite Shania's hopes that this video, which had a traditional, old-fashioned feel, would spur album sales and airtime, the video fell short of Top 40 status, as did her third video, for the single "You Lay a Whole Lot of Love on Me."

Mercury was not getting what it hoped for from its star to be, but the company had not yet abandoned Shania. In an attempt to pump up new interest, Luke Lewis, who had just taken over as president of the label, developed a new concept called Triple Play. The idea was to package three up-and-coming talents into one to introduce them to more radio time and fan exposure. Shania was bundled with a former rocker named John Brannen and with Toby Keith, a formidable honky-tonk baritone, garbed in a cowboy hat.

The trio embarked on a 15-city U.S. tour in the South and Southwest. Presumably these were areas of high interest in country music. Without a recognizable star to anchor it, however, the tour failed. It often seemed as if music industry executives were the only ones paying attention to the performers. Brannen faded from the country scene after his debut album. Keith fared better, snagging the lion's share of media attention during the tour. He has enjoyed subsequent success.

For Shania, the Triple Play was a resounding flop. Her career appeared to be spiraling downward toward obscurity. But out of the blue came another fateful phone call that would change Shania's life.

Since Shania was on tour, Mary Bailey took the call. She didn't recognize the caller's name, Robert John Lange. He had a British accent and said he was a record producer. Mary took his London address and heard him say that everyone called him "Mutt." She sent him a press kit, a copy of the debut CD, and an autographed black-and-white 8 x10 glossy photo of Shania. Mary assumed he was just another fan. She forgot about the call and went about her business.

When it came to Shania, however, Lange was persistent. He called again and wanted to talk personally to Shania. Mary promised she would take care of it. When she told Shania about Lange, Shania thought he was just a song-writer who was a fan. Her world and that of Lange's were much different. Shania had never heard of him. Luke Lewis knew of Lange, however, and he filled in the blanks for Shania and her manager.

Robert John "Mutt" Lange is known as one of the few superproducers in the rock music world. Monster hits like AC/DC's *Back in Black* and *Highway to Hell*, Def Leppard's "Pour Some Sugar on Me," and Bryan Adams's "Everything I Do (I Do for You)" are a mere sample of the albums and songs he has produced. Lange has also aided the careers of Foreigner, Michael Bolton, Billy Ocean, and the Cars.

Shania has recalled that she "had no idea he was a world-famous record producer." She said, "I didn't read the back of pop and rock albums, which was good because I wasn't intimidated by him. Otherwise, I don't think I would have been able to express myself creatively without any inhibitions. It worked out really well."

According to one report, Lange actually discovered Shania while watching Country Music Television (CMT) on its European satellite network from his home in London. Although a rock and pop producer, Lange enjoyed country music, and he caught Shania's video *What Made You Say That?* Intrigued with Shania's voice and poise, he knew he had to get in touch with her.

Whatever the story, the two finally connected on the phone. When Lange asked Shania to sing for him, she propped the phone on a pillow and crooned some songs.

Canadian Bryan Adams was just one of the singers whose music Robert "Mutt" Lange produced. Lange, who saw Shania's potential, used his experience and influence to help launch the young singer to the heights of music stardom.

Lange knew Shania's album, and he was curious about why she didn't record her own music on the disk. Flattered that he was interested in her songwriting, she sang "Home Ain't Where His Heart Is (Anymore)." A perceptive producer who knew talent when he heard it, Lange decided he had to talk more with Shania. For the next few weeks they talked music and ideas by phone. She sang for him; he played songs for her, including "I Said

I Loved You but I Lied," which would become a hit for pop-soul singer Michael Bolton. They exchanged songs they had written via Federal Express.

For Shania and Lange, their phone friendship was satisfying and creative. But they had to meet before long. The opportunity came at the Nashville Fan Fair in June 1993. The Fan Fair draws thousands of country music fans each year for its combination of concerts, parties, autograph sessions, and souvenir sales. Although not a smashing success, Shania had a booth at the fair, and she thoroughly enjoyed the fun and excitement. She couldn't believe her eyes when her phone friend Mutt Lange appeared at the booth. She was so elated, she gave the man she had never met personally a big hug. "I was so happy to meet him," she said. "He comes across as so warm, I knew we were going to be best friends."

Following the fair, Shania and Lange continued to keep in touch. They felt that it was inevitable they should collaborate and share their musical ideas. Both knew they wanted to produce their own album, with their own songs. In late 1993, the couple flew to Europe for what they called a "working" trip to start writing their songs. Both seemed to know, however, that the trip would be more than that. When Shania and Lange arrived in Paris, he popped the question. "I knew it was coming," Shania said. "He invited my sisters along, and I thought, 'That's kind of weird,' and he said, 'Well, I'm going to be working all the time, and I don't want you to be bored and alone.'" Shania's sister Carrie-Ann also saw what was coming. She recalled, "It was almost like he was getting on one knee and saying to us, 'Is it okay if I marry your sister?'"

It certainly was okay with everyone concerned, and they all hopped a plane back to Canada. On December 28, 1993, 28-year-old Shania Twain and 51-year-old Robert Lange were married in Huntsville, Ontario. With Lange at her side, Shania felt a tremendous fulfillment in

The Eiffel Tower looms over the city of Paris, the scene of Shania and Lange's trip to work on her music. Their musical collaboration turned into a personal one when Lange proposed marriage and Shania accepted.

her personal life. Her professional life, however, was stalled. It was time to bring Lange onto the recording scene and try to create music that would showcase the couple's own creativity.

With the help of her husband, Shania Twain was about to embark on a whole new era in her life.

Shania rehearses for her performance at the 1995 American Music Awards show in Los Angeles. Not only did she perform at the gala, she was nominated for three awards. With her successful album The Woman in Me *and the spin-off singles, Shania was at last reaching her goal of being one of the best, and most popular, country singers ever.*

4

THE WOMAN IN ME

SHANIA TWAIN'S LIFE has been more or less an open book. In contrast, Mutt Lange's career is something of a mystery. One account has it that he began his work in the 1970s with a San Francisco band called Clover, whose members included a harmonica player named Huey Lewis. Lewis later formed the well-known Huey Lewis and the News, which became one of the most popular bands of the 1980s. Lange wrote Lewis's "Do You Believe in Love?" Other sources report that Lange began his career in 1976 with his production of Graham Parker's *Heat Treatment*.

Three years later, Lange produced AC/DC's *Highway to Hell* album. His real claim to fame, however, is his 1980 production *Back in Black* for AC/DC. That recording—which included the hit "You Shook Me All Night Long"—exceeded the 10-million mark in sales. It was one of four albums Lange produced for the band fronted by singer Brian Johnson and guitarist brothers Angus and Malcolm Young.

From 1981 through 1987, Lange was the moving force behind myriad hit songs and albums, including Foreigner's 1981 megahit *4*, which earned Lange a Grammy nomination for Producer of the Year. Through the 1980s, he produced countless memorable tunes and continued to back rock groups.

It wasn't until 1991 that Lange showed up again with the release of his next production, Bryan Adams's *Waking Up the Neighbors* album. Lange continued working infrequently as the decade progressed. Def Leppard's Lange-produced 1992 effort, *Adrenalize*, was a crushing disappointment, critically and commercially. Nevertheless, in 1994 the American Society of Composers, Authors and Publishers (ASCAP) proclaimed Lange Songwriter of the Year.

Oddly, while Lange's list of credits goes on and on, little is known publicly about the production wizard. He shuns publicity and refuses to do interviews or to be photographed. He has never appeared to accept his awards, nor has he accompanied his wife to accept her accolades at public ceremonies. Lange asks the artists he works with not to include him in photographs of the sessions. Some musicians who have worked with Lange in the studio have even reported that they were required to sign privacy agreements, documents prohibiting them from divulging any personal information about the producer. Yet, despite his stern and fervent vigilance over his privacy, others have described him as "amiable and forthcoming" to those with whom he surrounds himself.

Reportedly, Lange was born the son of a blue-collar gold and asbestos miner in South Africa, though Lange has British citizenship. He is about 6' tall, has a ruddy complexion, and wears his blond hair long and shaggy. Some accounts describe him as unkempt; others picture him as "an aging rock star" or a man with a "post-hippie" look. In contrast to the huge sounds he elicits on recordings, he is also said to be a quiet individual.

Shania too likes a certain amount of privacy, but she appears in sharp contrast to Lange. A striking 5'4" brunette, Shania doesn't shun publicity. She is, after all, a public figure. She likes to be photographed, and the camera loves her. She is fussy about her appearance, including her clothes, her hair, and her makeup. Shania's innate shyness has caused some to describe her as aloof. The couple's romance and marriage came as a surprise to many of Shania's friends. Mary Bailey commented that Shania was

Backing rock groups like AC/DC, shown here in concert, was one of Robert Lange's specialties. People wondered if Lange could be successful in producing country music. With The Woman in Me, *he and Shania proved that he could.*

"very quiet, very reserved, and very cautious about who she lets in."

Before Lange entered the picture, Mercury had not yet given Shania a commitment for a second album. With the rock producer on board, however, the company was once again enthusiastic about the possibilities. But there was a catch. Lange was one of the most expensive producers in the business. He had had phenomenal success, but tapping that track record would cost money. Determined to make the album, Lange proposed a special deal, which Mercury jumped at. Lange would assume as much of the risk as the company if the project fizzled. He also waived his usual asking price.

In 1994, Shania and Lange began working on the singer's second album, to be titled *The Woman in Me.* The couple's romance and marriage happened in less than a year. But their joint album took more than a year to put together. Shania admitted that she knew the album would break some Nashville rules. But it was a labor of love, and producer Luke Lewis agreed. "You can feel the love that's in that album. They spent an awfully long time, compared to most albums in Nashville." Lewis had heard the music while the project was ongoing, and he was convinced that it would be a smash success. He did have some qualms, however. As he explained, "There was a question about whether the gadgeteers in the industry—the program directors and so on—were going to accept it. There was no doubt that it was sort of fringe, it was pushing the envelope in terms of what was going on in country music."

Initial resistance from the staid country music establishment to the Lange-produced Shania Twain album amounted to a virtual radio blackout. Many in the industry reportedly viewed the couple as trespassers, outsiders, and interlopers. Industry insiders like Norro Wilson countered the attacks. In an interview he described the reaction: "'What is a Mutt Lange? Who is a Mutt Lange?

And what has Mutt Lange done?' was the response from industry insiders. I didn't know. Next thing you know, here's a guy who has produced more albums on his own, probably, than if you took all our producers and put them together for a total."

Lange's anonymity was the result of his fierce need for privacy in his personal life. Indeed, after he and Shania married, their lives were somewhat shrouded in mystery. They took a secluded estate in the Adirondack Mountains in upstate New York, completely equipped with a recording studio. They have since sold that property and relocated to Switzerland. Ironically, the couple's desire to live a quiet, normal life has been constantly thwarted by the magnitude of Shania's musical successes.

Released in January 1995, *The Woman in Me* contained 12 songs, 10 of them written by Shania and Lange, including the title song, "The Woman in Me (Needs a Man Like You)," and the first song to be released as a single, "Whose Bed Have Your Boots Been Under?" The songs reflect a range of themes, from ballads of fading love "Home Ain't Where His Heart Is (Anymore)" to "Any Man of Mine," an anthem to the independence of young women. "(If You're Not in It for Love) I'm Outta Here" blends the singer's sultry voice with loud drums and a strong blues-guitar line. The video that accompanied this last number was an instant hit.

The Woman in Me was the breakthrough that Shania needed to make the industry take notice; it propelled her to the top of the charts and to country music stardom. Shania was invited to appear and perform at industry events, including the prestigious annual American Music Awards. On January 27, 1995, she wowed the audience with her voice and style. Adding to her pleasure at entertaining was the thrill of being nominated for three awards. She didn't get all three, but she did garner the Favorite New Country Artist Award.

The smash album cost more than $500,000 to produce.

While that figure is said to be 5 to 10 times bigger than the budgets for most country music albums, the amount is probably a fraction of what it would have cost had Lange not made the special offer to Mercury. The deal turned out well for everyone, however. Had it not, Mercury wouldn't have lost much but no doubt would have dropped Shania. And the singer would probably have faded into obscurity with a disastrous second album. After all, if she couldn't make a hit with Lange at the helm, could she ever? Shania's philosophical comment was, "If you're going to fall on your face, then you're going to fall on your face. It's a chance you have to be willing to take, and I was certainly willing to take that."

It was a gamble that paid off. Shania's run on the singles chart with songs from *The Woman in Me* spanned well over 100 weeks, and it was accomplished without a major concert tour, one of the commonly expected prerequisites for industry success. Still, Shania had to stand up to adversity when critics assumed her success was the result of Lange's studio magic, not her own talent. Once again, she needed to establish her own musical identity.

Despite his obvious contributions to her sound, Lange encouraged Shania's genuine talent to shine. His influence also extended beyond her music when he created a Shania image as well. Famed photographer John Derek—husband of model and actress Bo Derek—was hired to capture that image on film and direct the video for "Whose Bed Have Your Boots Been Under?" The video featured Shania in a sexy outfit singing to a host of oblivious men in a rural diner setting. Shania had been working on that particular song before she even met Lange. As he predicted, it became a hit, peaking at number 11 on *Billboard*'s country chart and eventually earning a gold certification.

With all of its polished production and professional packaging, *The Woman in Me* initially met with some critical disdain. Alanna Nash, a country music reviewer for *Entertainment Weekly*, gave the album an F and called it "one of the worst records of the decade." Nash jokingly wrote of Shania and Lange as "a former Canadian resort singer with a Karen Carpenter fixation" and "an over-the-top producer who thinks it would be fun to work in country."

Nash's opinion was only one, and *The Woman in Me* began climbing the charts. In the summer of 1995, the album and its singles finally began to catch hold within the country music industry. Country music critic Robert K. Oermann later told an interviewer that "Whose Bed Have Your Boots Been Under?" was "nearly lost in a radio blackout. It was a bare-knuckled brawl to get those people to play Twain's early Mutt Lange productions, because they were so different."

When it came to the videos, however, fans were grabbing them up. Luke Lewis was not sure just why the videos were so popular. "I'm not sure what hot buttons we pushed with the videos we made. Country music was very provincial at the time, it always has been." But he added, "[Shania] was more tapped in, probably, with the mainstream of America and what their tastes were and what they would tolerate, than any record company or anyone who programmed a radio station."

Shania seemed to be quite aware of the impact of her videos. She spent a great deal of money on producing them, and she was puzzled by the criticism that baring her midriff attracted. She started talking publicly about her feelings. "I think that the industry seriously underestimated the fans and where they were at," she has said. "I mean, come on, we have the internet these days. Watch TV for an hour! The times are very progressive and very free. That's why I don't particularly pay a lot of attention to what the industry is doing. I don't want to be influenced by it; I don't want to know what they consider right and wrong."

The singer went on to praise the fans for their tastes in music and videos. She contended they were real people who had real lives and they wanted real music and real words and thoughts. She especially wanted to send a message to young women to be comfortable with their bodies and not to try to hide them.

Robert K. Oermann was still offering his opinion when he surfaced again with his notion that Shania attracted the young people who frequented dance clubs and watched videos. These fans, he said disdainfully, had propelled her to stardom.

Oermann's sniping at Shania's music and success had little effect on her fans. Obviously they were not concerned about whether she was packaged or not. For the millions who snapped up the album and video, it was her voice and songs that counted. In the end the fans were the real critics. Shania was even competing with another famous Canadian. In Quebec, the home province of singer Celine Dion, *The Woman in Me* became the top-selling album.

Nor did Shania's appearances and performances show any signs of slacking off. At the 1995 Nashville Fan Fair in June, her booth was mobbed by fans who wanted to see their favorite singer. Two months later, Shania appeared to cohost a music festival north of Toronto. When she belted out "Any Man of Mine," fans went wild, clamoring for autographs and asking her to pose for photos with them.

In the fall of 1995, Shania was rushing from one appearance to another. October found her opening the Country Music Association Awards show in Nashville. The next month she performed at the annual Presidential Gala at Ford's Theater in Washington, D.C., where she met President Bill Clinton and First Lady Hillary Rodham Clinton. On Thanksgiving Day, New Yorkers were treated to Shania when she rode in the annual Macy's Thanksgiving Day parade. And as the year closed, still in New York, she

Performing live in Nashville is every country singer's dream. Shania fulfilled hers when she opened the 1995 Country Music Association Awards show in the heartland of country music.

Shania had a banner year in 1995. Here, she is greeted by First Lady Hillary Rodham Clinton at a presidential gala.

sang at the *Billboard* Music Awards on December 6. At one point she was asked how this frantic schedule affected her relationship with Mutt. She answered, "I've been so busy, we usually pass each other at airports."

Still, Nashville did not let up. Rumors circulated that Lange had bought radio time and lined up advertising deals to ensure the success of Shania's album. There was even a rumor that he had personally purchased a huge quantity of the recording to bolster its sales figures and make it appear a bigger hit than it really was.

Whatever triggered the momentum, Shania's popularity took off. "My head is spinning," she told one interviewer during the explosion of her popularity. Such a rapid rise to fame had occurred only one time before in the history of the country music industry—in 1990, when Garth Brooks released his *No Fences* album.

In 1996, Shania was traveling the sometimes rocky road to fame. She was criticized for not touring to promote her album and songs, and controversy swirled around her early life. But her fans, to whom she gives a thumbs-up sign here, flocked to her appearances, and The Woman in Me *and her singles were riding high on the charts.*

5

THE ROAD
TO FAME

IN AUGUST 1995, Shania was appearing at a Mercury-Nashville event at Laguna Beach, California, with a band she had put together. Just as she was about to begin her gig, Luke Lewis announced that she would not tour to promote *The Woman in Me*. Shania's decision was something of a shock and provoked a good deal of controversy, further fueling the notion that she was a studio creation. Her many live performances should have dispelled that notion. But critics weighed in once again.

Country music critic Robert K. Oermann was stunned that Shania stayed off the road when her record was taking off. For Shania, touring didn't appear to be necessary. *The Woman in Me* rose to sales of more than 13 million copies by 1996. But Shania wasn't sitting still, either. She took every opportunity to make appearances without performing. She went to autograph signings, attended special fan functions, appeared on slick magazine covers, and gave interviews. In February 1996, she appeared to a crowd of some 20,000 at the

Mall of America in Minneapolis. She didn't sing a word but just signed autographs. In fact, with Lange as her mentor, Shania was taking control of her own career. She had learned a lesson from the failure of her first album. She was determined that would not happen again.

Though offers came in for tours, Shania Twain initially refused. She reasoned that the time wasn't yet right. She didn't want to compete as a show. And she was not about to follow the traditional route of performing as an opening act for established country artists. Even when Shania was offered equal billing with Wynonna Judd and Reba McEntire, she resisted. As a result a critical backlash ensued. Critics speculated that maybe she couldn't sing live with the same presence she had in a studio. Perhaps, they said, she really was a creation of Mutt Lange, just an enhanced voice in front of a multilayered wall of sound he created with track after track of recording. Maybe she had no idea how to bring the music to life on stage.

Shania held her ground, however. She refused to give in to the temptation to tour just to prove her critics wrong. She continued spending most of her time on well-planned appearances with her fans. Just meeting with her admirers seemed to be enough to keep her momentum at full steam.

Nothing, it seemed, would dampen Shania's popularity. As 1996 got under way, she was once again a star attraction at music industry events. At the American Music Awards in January, Shania was in the company of such country greats as Garth Brooks and Reba McEntire. By that time, Shania had been riding *Billboard*'s Top Country Albums chart for 29 weeks, breaking McEntire's record.

The audience at the awards roared with approval as Shania performed. But it wasn't just her vocal talent that entranced them. Shania's costume broke all the unwritten rules about how a country star should dress. Skintight vinyl pants with a halter to match and spiked heels was just not "country." Costume or not, she picked up the

Favorite New Country Artist Award at the ceremony.

Shania was not neglected by the Grammys either. In February, she performed at the event in Los Angeles and was also a presenter. Nominated for four awards, she won for Best Country Album. Blockbuster Entertainment Awards followed up by handing Shania its Favorite Country Artist Award in March. In April, *The Woman in Me* garnered Shania the Top New Female Vocalist and Album of the Year awards from the Academy of Country Music. A live concert with Alvin Chea of Take 6 followed in May.

And the rising star's success was going ahead full steam. *The Woman in Me* and its singles continued to soar on the charts in 1996. Several songs, including "The Woman in Me" and "(If You're Not in It for Love) I'm Outta Here" topped the charts for more than 20 weeks. When "Home Ain't Where the Heart Is (Anymore)" and the lullaby-hymn "God Bless the Child" were released, the proceeds were donated to Kids Cafe/Second Harvest

Despite her critics, Shania's success and popularity increased. Here, Shania reacts to winning the trophy for Favorite New Country Artist from the American Music Awards in January 1996. To accept the award, she had donned a jacket over her black vinyl outfit.

Food Bank in the United States, and in Canada to the Canadian Living Foundation, which provides meals for underprivileged children.

The 10 songs composed by Shania and Lange were in stark contrast to Shania's writing credit on her first album. Many critics initially theorized that the rock elements so evident on the recording were simply Lange's honing of Shania's raw country material. Shania soundly disputed those conclusions. She noted that it was Lange who pushed for the dominant steel guitar and fiddle sounds on the album. It was his love of country music, she contended. Still, it is hard to hear some elements in Shania's songs and not recall the big-drummed, arena-rock anthems of the 1980s.

With Lange's support and encouragement, Shania's fairy tale had come true. With success, however, came pressure. The media was eager to know more about the woman who was selling so many albums without taking to the road. Though Shania had never set out to capitalize on her childhood poverty, the tragic loss of her parents, and the responsibilities she faced thereafter, reporters insisted on pestering her. Shania had managed to hide many details from the public relations people at Mercury and subsequently from her bio information. Sooner or later, however, a more accurate picture was sure to come out. When it did, journalists had a field day with it.

Rumors began to spread that she had been creating herself all along, and that her tragic but inspiring tale didn't add up. Writer Laurence Leamer, who wrote the gossipy *Kennedy Women,* suggested in his book *Three Chords and the Truth*, that Shania's tale was a "brilliant reconstruction . . . a virtual past."

In April 1996, another shot was fired from Shania's hometown newspaper, the *Timmins Daily Press.* In a front-page article, the newspaper reported, "The *Daily Press* has learned that Twain has woven a tapestry of half-truths and outright lies in her climb to the top of the country charts."

The article quoted her biological father, Clarence Edwards, who had claimed a paternal connection with his now-famous long-lost daughter. Shania has steadfastly maintained that Jerry Twain is the only man she ever considered as her father, since Edwards apparently abandoned his family when she was only two years old. The *Daily Press* article also questioned both her Native American heritage and her paternity. Shania remains adamant and stands behind her account. She has repeated again and again that she was adopted into a Native American community by her stepfather.

In a written response to the newspaper, Shania made it clear that she never had a connection to her biological father. "Although I was briefly introduced to Clarence a couple of times in my teen years," she wrote, "I never knew him growing up. . . . I never felt the need to seek the love or support of another family because I had it from the Twains." When Shania threatened to sue the

Rumors and gossip surrounding Shania's family and her Native American heritage did not send her into seclusion. Shrugging them off, she continued her appearances, including this performance with Alvin Chea of the group Take 6.

newspaper, it printed a front-page retraction expressing its sincere regrets over any suggestion that Shania had lied.

Twain also explained to the *Los Angeles Daily News*, "It's ridiculous to have this [Edwards] family try to claim me back. Our struggle ever since my parents died was to stay grounded and anchored as a family. This new development is like a divider. It's kind of late to try and claim me." She also fired her own shot at the media: "Of course, the media wants something to be hidden. They want me to have a skeleton in my closet. But I really don't have any."

The smear seems a moot issue today, given the obvious fact that most of her fans really don't seem to care as much about her background. They are enthralled with her look and her sound. It's hard to imagine that the millions of people who have bought her CDs and tickets to her concerts did so because she was raised in an Ojibwa setting. Still, the accusations hurt. Shania was stung by both the allegations that she was less than honest and the attacks on her relationship with Jerry Twain. Nothing, she insists, is contrived about her career.

While she seems to have set that gossip to rest, Shania has had other family problems. She has been troubled by the behavior of her siblings and their run-ins with the law. Her younger sister, Carrie-Ann, was arrested for trying to burn down a boyfriend's house in Timmins. Her brothers, Mark and Darryl, were arrested for driving under the influence of alcohol in 1996. The following year, Mark Twain was charged for breaking the window of his girlfriend's car, assaulting a police officer, and resisting arrest. Both brothers were also later arrested in Huntsville, Ontario, for attempting to steal cars, an episode that resulted in a six-month jail term for Mark.

For ordinary people these charges would barely be worthy of the police blotter sections of most newspapers. Since they concern the relatives of a superstar, however, they have been highly publicized. Of these episodes, Shania has refused to speak publicly, deeming them private. Still, Shania was shocked when she realized how her fame made scandal profitable for the media. Her brothers, who now work in the woods cutting timber, also suffer from the knowledge that their actions have hurt their sister. Shania has said in explanation, "It's difficult for them to be exposed if they do anything wrong . . . but at the same time, it helps keep them straight. I guess you know you've made a certain level when you make the tabloids."

The revelations about Shania's background and the gossip that surrounded her didn't have much influence on the people of Timmins, Ontario. She was still their home-town hero. In August they showed their loyalty and their pride in her success by honoring her with the keys to the city and dedicating a garden to her. Thousands of town-folks turned out on a dreary, rainy day to greet her. Crowds of fans followed Shania and town officials to the guitar-shaped flower garden named in her honor. As part of the ceremonies, Shania planted a tree in honor of her grandfather and her parents. "This," she said, "is a symbol of replacing some of what we take from nature." For Shania, it was an emotional day, and the tabloid stories seemed to fade into the background.

Shania may have come to the conclusion that it is dif-ficult, and sometimes impossible, to control the actions of others, especially relatives. People should be judged for their own actions, not those of their relatives. One of those actions by Shania herself may leave some of her fans wondering what their favorite star is really like.

In November 1996, it was reported that Shania fired her longtime friend and manager, Mary Bailey, with a tele-phone call. All ties with the woman she had described as a mentor and "like a mother" to her were severed. Shania completely cut off the woman who had done so much to give her success and stardom. Although Mary has admitted to being deeply hurt, even shattered, she has steadfastly refrained from publicly saying anything overtly negative

Shania's hometown of Timmins has always remained loyal to its celebrated singing star. She proudly shows off the key to the city on her visit in August 1996. Timmins also honored Shania by declaring August 15 Shania Twain Day.

about the woman she looked on as a daughter. When questioned about Mary's ousting, Shania responded in an offhand manner, painting the query as "old news." She said only that she had "moved on," telling the *Toronto Star*, "Change is normal. I like to go forward."

For Twain, going forward meant signing with Landau Management, headed by Jon Landau, who had represented Bruce Springsteen for more than 20 years. Shania's relationship with Landau Management would lead to yet another stage in her career.

Shania finally went on a concert tour to support her third album. Come on Over, *a salute to women, became a smash hit that surpassed even the success of the immensely popular* The Woman in Me, *catapulting the singer to new heights of stardom.*

6

SUCCESS AND
ACCOLADES

AFTER SHANIA'S INCREDIBLE success with *The Woman in Me*, she and Mutt set out to create another smash hit. At their home nestled in New York State's Adirondack Mountains, they settled in to write and arrange their music. Shania described how they worked: "I sat down and wrote the songs and the ideas for the songs that I had," she said. "Then I got with Mutt and collaborated on what we had." As they wrote and arranged, the couple came up with a score of songs, actually more than could be squeezed into one album. And they worked at a slow pace, without pressure. Shania and Mutt could take their time to create the songs they believed in. According to Shania, she and Mutt never felt that there was a point at which they had to rush to finish.

By the summer of 1997, Shania and Mutt were giving Mercury executives a taste of the album, titled *Come on Over*. Mercury was enthusiastic about the songs and began a campaign to promote the album's release. To begin, the company released the first single from the album,

"Love Gets Me Every Time," in September. It quickly climbed *Billboard*'s Country Singles Chart to number 29, the highest ever for a debut single by a female country artist. When *Come on Over* was finally released in November 1997, it featured 16 songs cowritten by Shania and Lange and sung by Shania. The reviews were glowing, justifying Shania's faith in her artistry and her partnership with her husband. *Billboard* magazine wrote:

> In attempting to live up to the expectations created by the remarkable success of her last album, *The Woman in Me*, Shania Twain and her collaborator/producer Mutt Lange have successfully created the same thing, only more so. Not the same album, but the same sorts of unexpected turns, the same punchy pop country. These 16 songs (totaling just over an hour) reflect the day-to-day preoccupations, interests and concerns of a young woman: her takes on the many twists of life and love. In translating those into modern country, Twain and Lange continue to test the limits of country music and sometimes go far beyond them. In a very real sense, this is the future of power pop merging with country. In the process, country's traditions are being reinvented and redefined.

In *Come on Over*, Shania was raising her fist in salute to women. As she had in the past, she based many of her lyrics on the rebellious woman who has found freedom in asserting herself. Lyrics such as these from "Honey, I'm Home" allowed her fans to identify with her strong feminine mystique.

> The car won't start—it's falling apart.
> I was late for work and the boss got smart.
> My pantyline shows—got a run in my hose.
> My hair went flat—man, I hate that (I hate that)
> I broke a nail opening the mail.
> I cursed out loud 'cause it hurt like hell.
> This job's a pain—it's so mundane.
> It sure don't stimulate my brain.

Such lyrics may be today's version of another country classic—Johnny Paycheck's "Take This Job and Shove It." But yesterday's country stars didn't sing about such things as panty lines and breaking nails. Shania may have been intentionally puncturing the stereotype of men who expect women to wait on them when they come home from a hard day at work. But she also makes it quite clear that her message goes far beyond that.

The song "Black Eyes, Blue Tears," which bridges with the line, "I'd rather die standing/Than live on my knees, begging please . . ." ends with the spoken verse: "Find your self-esteem and be forever free to dream." Shania's battle cry for battered women shows another side of her iron-will feminine image. "If You Want to Touch Her, Ask!" sends a call to popular culture to respect women. "Don't Be Stupid (You Know I Love You)" attacks the spirit of suspicion and jealousy that often precipitates violence against women. But "That Don't Impress Me Much" lightens the tone while giving the woman power well above that of the man.

Tempering the album is one of Shania's biggest hits ever, "You're Still the One," which proclaims that love can endure and survive against all odds. Shania is saying that while women must overcome bad relationships and circumstances, they can also use their power to preserve good ones.

The anthem "Man! I Feel Like a Woman!" painted Shania as a feminist crusader. But it was "Rock This Country" that put her over the top with both men and women. The song invites anyone who will listen to let the good times roll with lines like "Every brown-eyed boy—every blue-eyed girl/Gotta really go psycho— give it a whirl. . . ." With this tune, fans identified with their own desires to be less restrained and to cut loose, whether they are country music lovers or pop and rock boppers. The infectious, driving rhythm of the song

A sold-out audience in Sudbury, Ontario, is treated to Shania's songs and energetic performance style. The occasion was a kick-off concert for a worldwide tour, which she had decided on with the success of her third album.

propels it with turbocharged release, and then Shania boldly exclaims:

We're pluggin' in the power
Crankin' up the sound
It's comin' your direction
It's headin' to your town
We're kickin' up the dust
Blowin' off the steam
Let's get nuts now
Everybody scream!

Shania opens the album to the women of the world with the invitation "Let's go, girls" and then leads them down a path of fun-loving abandon in "Man! I Feel Like a Woman!" with lines like these:

No inhibitions—make no conditions
Get a little outta line
I ain't gonna act politically correct
I only wanna have a good time.

Evidently, the singer's lyrics also excited feelings in the executives at Revlon. In the summer of 1999 the words "Let's go, girls" and the telltale opening electric fiddle riff of "Man! I Feel Like a Woman!" were first heard on television as preambles to lively ads for Revlon's cosmetics.

The mammoth firm added the now internationally recognized star to its roster of glamorous spokespersons. Shania was standing shoulder to shoulder with the likes of Cindy Crawford, Halle Berry, and Melanie Griffith. Shania's debut with the firm corresponded with the U.S. launch of Revlon's newest breakthrough product, ColorStay Liquid Lip. She was featured in several of the company's print and television advertising campaigns and supported a broad range of promotional activities. Her first advertising campaign for Liquid Lip broke into the airwaves with a commercial featuring her award-winning "Man! I Feel Like a Woman!"

Both print and television campaigns somewhat re-created the video clip she had recorded for the song, which was a parody of Robert Palmer's breakthrough video of his hit, "Addicted to Love." Palmer had featured himself in a suit crooning in front of a band of women musicians in identical costumes and hairstyles who gyrated to music they poorly pretended to be playing. Shania's video had her in dress clothing with a heavy dose of makeup strutting in front of a muscle-bound, all-male band. After all, she proclaims in the song, "The best thing about being a woman/Is the prerogative to have a little fun. . . ."

In addition to the strong, proud lyrics on *Come on Over*, the album once again bore an eclectic brew of Lange's trademark sounds. The chorus of "Honey, I'm Home," with its "hey, oh hey" call-and-response techniques, slamming drums, and powerful guitar slides, makes it easy to overlook its nondistorted fiddles and steel guitar elements. Listeners could almost think of it as another version of Def Leppard's "Pour Some Sugar on Me" or just about anything else from the band's *Hysteria* album. Even with the steel guitar and the fiddles, the album sounded even less country than its predecessor.

With the international splash Shania had made in the music industry in general, it no longer mattered what she called herself. Country, pop, rock—she could have billed herself as a polka peddler and she would have likely sold piles of albums. Mercury Records, along with the country music business itself, had also seen a glimmer of the big picture, and it wasn't about to look away. Who would dare disclaim one of the biggest rising stars in the world? Not only did Shania now rule the charts, videos from the album's singles were still in hot rotation on Country Music Television and MTV. To top it all, Shania's songs were pretty much the sound track for just about every county fair across the United States.

Despite her image as a sexy young woman with

Thanks to the overwhelming success of Come on Over *and its appeal to women of all ages, Shania was tapped as spokesperson for Revlon cosmetics. Joining the ranks of other celebrities, her glamorous image appeared widely in the company's print and television ads.*

leopard-print clothes and an exposed navel, Shania is in reality quite conservative. When she shot the video for "Man! I Feel Like a Woman!" she sported a very short skirt. Underneath, she was wearing shorts. "I'm still very conservative when I'm not performing," she has said. "Like on the beach I don't like people looking at my body." That same attitude is part of her songwriting. She told an interviewer in December 1999 that her songs are not deeply personal or autobiographical. She said, "I'm not that dramatic. I don't feel the need to communicate my innermost feelings—and they wouldn't get it, so what's the point. I only want to release music that people relate to. That's my thrill."

With the completion of *Come on Over,* Shania turned her attention to her maiden tour, beginning in 1998. She was about to prove wrong all those critics who had accused her of being a studio creation as she literally exploded onto the touring scene. The tour spanned some 60 appearances, complete with pyrotechnics, monster Jumbo-Tron video screens, and myriad costume changes. They weren't the typical stand, sing, strum, and wave concerts for which country music was known. Starting in Sudbury, Ontario, Shania injected her live performances with the over-the-top aspects of monumental rock shows, including a band that reflected her nontraditional style.

"I don't want a show that's over-produced," Shania told an interviewer. "There will be great lights, excellent sound and a band that's animated, and the live arrangements of songs will be a big part of the dynamics of the show. But it won't be as slick as a Janet Jackson show. Now [with the release of *Come on Over*], I have enough songs to do a proper length show with original material." She added, "You can't be a headlining act and get up and do only six songs. I never wanted to be in a position of having to fill the gaps. As a songwriter, that would have been insulting to me."

While Lange made a rare public appearance by manning the soundboard for her debut show, Shania insisted that she was involved in every aspect of the production. "We're offering the best in light and sound, but the music will always be first. We've been arranging the songs so they'll fit better into a live setting. They're slightly different arrangements, but everybody will know the songs. We actually had to cut the show down from two-and-a-half hours to two hours. We wanted people to get home before midnight," she explained.

Another thing Shania did on her tour for her fans was to reserve a few seats in the front to bring people down from top sections. She claimed that the top, back rows

were the only places from which she had ever viewed a concert as a spectator, and she wanted some of her fans to know the thrill of seeing a show up close. She also brought in a choir of local singers from each town she played to back her up on her single "God Bless the Child."

Another of her personal touches on the giant production was handpicking the opening acts. For the start of the tour, she tapped another Canadian group, Leahy. A Celtic-oriented pop act from Lakefield, Ontario, Leahy warmed up the crowds with lively Irish-style fiddling and step dancing.

Country music critic Robert K. Oermann was on hand again to give a thumbs up for the show. Oermann was impressed with the audience, commenting, "It wasn't just

With all her success and renown, Shania never forgot her fans. And they did not forget her, flocking to enjoy concerts on her worldwide tour. Here, Shania greets a young fan and autographs a shirt.

a bunch of little Shania Spice Girl wannabes bouncing around in little outfits." The audience included listeners ranging from teenage boys to grandmothers, which made it clear that Shania was making modern country music accessible to everyone. Shania sang and pranced for two hours. Said one reviewer, "By any measure, whether you like her music or not, it is a vindication for her. There's something about her that I like, and not just physically. There's some grit there. She has a kind of steely determination about her. She's the girl in your high school class that got straight A's, not because she was the most gifted but because she studied really, really hard. And I like her for it."

These were accolades that Shania was finally getting used to. From the release of *The Woman in Me*, the singer has received scores of awards and honors in her stellar rise to fame. "I'm always excited when I win something," she declared in an interview. "Just to be nominated, of course, is fun. . . . It always brings a smile to my face. It's such a nice perk, and I appreciate it, but even if I win something, I'm not going to get so over the top about it. It's just—you can't." Over the top or not, Shania has plenty of reason to smile about her awards.

To put her honors in perspective, a comparison with another country music superstar shows that Shania has goals toward which she can still strive. The phenomenon known as Garth Brooks has sold more than 95 million albums since 1989, earning him the title of the highest-selling solo artist in music history. He has 43 career hits, and has set a record by earning 24 *Billboard* Music Awards. Brooks has also landed 16 ACMA Awards, 13 American Music Awards, 11 CMMA Awards, and 10 People's Choice Awards.

The pinnacle of music awards, however, is the Grammy. Brooks has won two in his career. Shania has landed three. Presented annually by the National Academy of Recording Arts and Sciences, the Grammys are the most coveted of

the many contemporary music awards. Nabbing a Grammy is the dream of every music artist. A Grammy is awarded by the academy to honor excellence in the recording arts and sciences, and it is truly a peer award, given by and to artists and technical professionals. Granting of the awards has nothing to do with sales or chart positions. Still, despite the honor the awards carry and the ratings success of the televised presentations, many industry insiders consider Grammys to be merely a reflection of

Garth Brooks, who has sold more albums than any other solo artist in history, is widely recognized for his country music artistry. Brooks has won two Grammys; by contrast, Shania Twain has won three.

At the pinnacle of her success, Shania received two Grammy Awards in 1999. Smiling and confident, she holds up her trophies for Best Country Album and Best Female Country Vocal.

mainstream commercial success. An international audience of more that 1.5 billion people in 170 countries tune in to broadcasts of the Grammys.

In addition to Grammys for artistic excellence, the academy also gives other awards that recognize contributions and activities of significance to the recording industry. These categories include the Lifetime Achievement Award, Trustees Award, Hall of Fame Award, Technical Grammy Award, and Grammy Legends Award.

Shania and Lange's joint 1998 Grammy Award was for Best Country Song for "You're Still the One." Shania performed the song at the awards ceremony held in February 1999. True to form, Lange did not attend. Shania also garnered a Grammy for Best Female Country Vocal Performance for the same song.

The annual Country Music Association Awards were presented in September 1999 at Nashville's Grand Ole Opry House. At that ceremony, Shania received the Entertainer of the Year honor. When the American Music Awards were announced in 2000, Shania claimed the Favorite Country Female Performer Award. It was her fourth such award from the association. She also won the 2000 Favorite Pop/Rock Female Performer Award from the AMA.

Shania did lose out at the 1999 *Billboard* Music Awards. She was in the company of such nominees as Garth Brooks, Madonna, Mariah Carey, Celine Dion, Whitney Houston, and Michael Bolton for the Artist of the Decade award, which went to Mariah Carey. An 18-year-old former "Mouseketeer," Britney Spears, beat Shania out in the Female Artist of the Year category.

Shania takes her losses philosophically. But then, she has so many wins. In an interview, she explained her attitude about awards, saying that she took them a lot more seriously when she was a fan. "I remember myself as a fan watching award shows, and getting bitterly disappointed when my favorite person didn't win and jumping for joy when my person won," she said. Apparently, when one has reached Shania's pinnacle of success, awards are not that important. After all, Shania knows what she has accomplished.

Seemingly oblivious to a pouring rain, Shania belts out one of her top-selling singles, "Honey, I'm Home." Her signature bare midriff and bold style are not always in sync with Nashville's country image, but Shania continues to captivate millions of fans.

7

BIGGER THAN LIFE

BY 1998, AFTER a mere five years as a recording artist, Shania Twain had become one of only five female performers to hit the 10-million sales mark. And *The Woman in Me*, as the fourth country album to reach 10 million sales, put her in the company of Garth Brooks and Willie Nelson.

Another grand indicator of Twain's enduring success and acceptance into stardom came in April 1998, when she was invited to perform at VH1's *Divas Live* concert—an intimate gathering that featured some of contemporary music's foremost singers. Twain sang alongside the legendary Aretha Franklin, as well as contemporary divas Celine Dion, Mariah Carey, and Gloria Estefan. An accompanying recording, *Divas Live*, was released in October 1998.

On January 7, 1999, Shania crossed the border into Canada for a brief visit to her hometown. She was in Timmins to do a two-day video shoot for her television special, "Shania Twain's Winter Break." Of course, the event caught the attention of the *Timmins*

One measure of Shania's success was sharing the stage with two music superstars. The occasion was the Divas Live concert in New York City, when Shania joined Celine Dion (left) and Gloria Estefan (center).

Daily Press. The paper said that the approximately 15-member television crew was intent on filming "a true representation of her Canadian background, which included snowmobiling and visiting her old haunts."

One of those haunts was the Maple Leaf Hotel. "Let me introduce you to the Maple Leaf," Twain announced before a crowd of about 100 excited onlookers at the Balsam Street South landmark. "I've had [a] great time writing songs about relationships between men and women, and it all started at a place like the Maple Leaf." The singer told her fans that her parents would take her to sing in places like the Maple Leaf when she was a child. Samantha Johnson, national publicity manager for Mercury Records, told the *Daily Press*, "[Shania] is very proud of her roots and very proud of Timmins being her hometown."

The two-day-long Timmins shoot took place during a five-week break in Shania's *Come On Over* world concert tour, which had begun in 1998. It was difficult, Shania said, to find the time to visit with hometown family and friends during the shoot, but she mentioned that she was eager to return for a concert date later in the year.

Naturally, the town of Timmins was excited. One of the onlookers that day, a local musician named Darrell Gould, told the newspaper, "It's not every day you get to stand beside a superstar. . . . She's bigger than life; she's every person's dream."

That dream came true for a lot more of her hometown's citizens when Shania kept her promise to return by scheduling a Canada Day (July 1) concert in Timmins later that year. More than 20,000 fans filled the town's Hollinger Park for the show, despite a bout of dismal weather. Shania enthused over the turnout, announcing that she was really excited that half the town was in attendance. "The support," she said, "is overwhelming." The singer also said that her band and crew were "moved and touched" by the affection people were showing for their native daughter.

Not everyone was from Timmins, however. Some journeyed many miles to see Shania perform. One fan, Mike Bourdon, said that he and his brother Stan had driven in from Hamilton, Ontario, a trek of more than 500 miles. Since it was raining, the two fans donned raincoats fashioned from garbage bags to watch the show. Mike Bourdon said, "This is the best place to see Shania perform, in her home town . . . rain or no rain."

Shania had actually arrived in Timmins three days before the show and had been staying at a camp outside of town. It seems she wanted to spend some time in her familiar woods. When Shania began her performance, the music could be heard throughout the downtown area. No one seemed to notice the rain, and city police reported that the crowd, which the *Timmins Daily Press* called "unprecedented" in size, gave them no problems.

Proceeds from the concert were donated to several local charitable organizations, including Matagami First Nations, the Timmins Community Partners for Child Nutrition/Breakfast for Learning programs, the Porcupine Food Bank, and the Timmins District Hospital. Shania had made several previous contributions to the food bank.

Shania closed the show with a chorus of "O Canada," the Canadian national anthem, backed by the crowd. The singing was followed by a fireworks display. The entire event was fitting, said the newspaper, for a Canada Day celebration.

The tour itself was not all glamour and glory, however. Shania became very depressed as the 14-month traveling show wore on. She felt terribly isolated and attributed her feelings of depression to the realization that she just didn't have as much freedom as she craved.

Shania tried to take back bits and pieces of her sanity while on the road by sneaking out on her own from time to time. She didn't tell anyone where she was going; she wanted no security or anyone keeping tabs on her. Sometimes she even entered a concert hall alongside her fans, who were oblivious to the fact that the star they came to see perform was actually standing incognito right next to them. She found that adventure exciting, getting away with being among the crowd and not being recognized.

Also, being away from Lange for so long made Shania feel disconnected. She talked to him on the phone, but she felt awkward because he wasn't really part of her daily life. When she commented publicly on these feelings, the tabloids picked up on it right away. They took some potshots at the separated couple, publishing unfounded rumors that they were breaking up. The *National Enquirer* reported that the couple was divorcing. The paper printed a story that while in Timmins, Shania ran into a boyfriend from the old days. When he saw

Shania, so the story went, he promptly left his wife and children. Divorce was inevitable. Lange shrugged off the allegations, but Shania was disturbed. "What bothers me most is that people take [the tabloids] seriously," she later commented in an interview.

Another myth about Shania and Lange's relationship was shattered when Danny Goldberg, the former head of Mercury Records Group, opened up in an interview. He described Lange as more experienced but brushed aside the opinions of many that Lange was totally in control of the situation. Goldberg said he realized after meeting the couple that Shania was Lange's equal, confiding that Lange was following Shania's lead. Luke Lewis also went public in an interview, calling the couple's relationship healthy. "They're both very forceful, bright people, and they respect each other . . . [Shania's] so controlled and focused, it's spooky. It's probably a throwback to being a hungry kid and not wanting to ever be hungry again," he added. "It almost becomes a curse, because you don't sit back and enjoy your success."

Shania may also have felt less than comfortable in her initial relationship with Lange because of the disparity between their finances. She was too cautious and disciplined to allow herself to enjoy life beyond her means. Lange didn't agree. He thought it was okay to spend. Shania has commented about that. "I worked my butt off, and now I'm financially independent. I can help my family with my money, give to charity with my money."

The star has given to charity, and she is also involved in a project in her hometown. She is excited about an interpretive center in Timmins and has donated more than $1 million in personal items, including the bejeweled black gown she wore to President Bill Clinton's inauguration and a tight-fitting dress created from old Dallas Cowboy football jerseys of quarterback Troy Aikman.

The site sprawls over 60 acres, with the Shania Twain Center to be the major attraction. Plans include interactive displays and a room dedicated to Shania's early days as a struggling artist in her hometown. She would also like to see a place for computer-enhanced instruments that visitors can play. Shania and the townspeople hope the center will boost tourism in Timmins.

However, helping to organize and support charities certainly can't fill the void of the couple's separations. Both are working artists. While Shania was on tour, Lange was supervising work on their new home in Switzerland and engineering projects with other artists.

Still, Shania could not seriously complain. *Come on Over* was rocking the world of country music, breaking all kinds of records along the way, and establishing her as a force to be reckoned with. Her first major tour also sold more than a million tickets worldwide.

With soaring record sales, sold-out performances, a place at the top of the charts, and piles of awards, one top honor still eluded Shania. She had not won a highly coveted award from the prestigious Country Music Association. Music critics, and her country music colleagues as well, were puzzled. As Nashville journalist Michael McCall commented, "She hasn't won the awards she should have. It hasn't quite happened for her as it has for Garth [Brooks] or the Dixie Chicks." Singer Reba McEntire agreed: "She's been at the top of the charts for two years and she still hasn't gotten the pats on the back that she deserves." Nashville, it seemed, still did not consider her country enough. Shania's crossover music was not traditional country, and her pop-rock songs and style seemed to offend the Nashville establishment.

Before the 1999 awards ceremony, however, Shania traveled to London in July to appear at a benefit sponsored by the British royal family. Two months later, she was in Nashville for the biggest event in country music. The ceremony included honors for country-music greats Dolly Parton, Conway Twitty, and Johnny Bond, who were inducted into the Country Music Hall of Fame.

Parton thrilled the audience with a rousing rendition of a bluegrass number, "Train, Train." Shania too performed, sporting a ten-gallon cowboy hat, boots, and short shorts—and with her signature bare midriff.

Many felt that Shania was a longshot for the major award of Entertainer of the Year since her rivals included such greats as Garth Brooks and George Strait. When the moment came and the winner was announced, Shania took the trophy, which she tearfully accepted from Reba McEntire. She had overcome the prejudice of traditional Nashville and had vindicated her music. As Vince Gill put it after her triumph, "Well, Shania, that might shut everybody up. You did it, baby."

Backstage, Shania spoke about her triumph: "This honor," she said, "comes mostly as a surprise, because I sort of convinced myself I wasn't going to win a thing. It's my first CMA. I don't resent not winning one before.

During her appearance in London at a benefit for the Prince's Trust in 1999, Shania chatted with Britain's Prince Charles.

I learned not to set myself up for disappointment whether I thought I deserved it or not. I was really prepared not to win." At a press conference, she also expressed her views on being a celebrity, claiming that the attention was great when it was positive and not negative. She also added, "As far as the actual fame goes, I don't like being treated like a star."

Whatever her feelings about stardom, however, Shania had reached the pinnacle with her music and especially with her third album.

Come on Over peaked at number two on *Billboard* magazine's music charts. November 1999 turned out to be a big month for Shania. Her native Canada honored her—and Lange—with three awards from the Society of Composers, Authors, and Music Publishers of Canada for the songs "You're Still the One," "From This Moment On," and "Don't Be Stupid" from *Come on Over*. She taped her second CBS network TV special in Dallas, Texas. "Shania Twain: Come on Over" aired on CBS on Thanksgiving evening, November 25. And she graced the cover of *Redbook* magazine's December issue. At the end of 1999, the album was in its 108th week on *Billboard*'s 200 chart. At the beginning of December 1999, it had jumped from number 24 to number 11— probably because of the Thanksgiving Day special on CBS—and earned the magazine's "Greatest Gainer" designation that week.

The Recording Industry Association of America (RIAA) certified Twain's *Come on Over* as 11 times platinum by early June 1999; it reached 12 million by late July and jumped to 13 million by late August. Her third album—the second-highest-selling album by a female artist in the history of the recording industry— reached a new milestone in November 1999, when its sales of 14 million were announced by the RIAA. At that time, she was trailing closely behind Alanis Morissette for the honor of all-time female sales leader.

Clad entirely in red, from her boots to her hat, Shania gives a stunning performance at the 1999 Country Music Association Awards. Facing competition from the Dixie Chicks, Garth Brooks, and George Strait, Shania ran off with the Entertainer of the Year Award.

Around that time, an international version of *Come on Over* was also released domestically in the United States. Mercury Records released the repackaged recording on November 23, which featured special versions of 15 of the 16 songs on the original release. The new international album also featured radio versions of four of her biggest pop hits: "You're Still the One," "From This Moment On,"

Not since 1986 had a woman won the Entertainer of the Year Award from the Country Music Association. Overcome with emotion and close to tears, Shania accepts the award from Reba McEntire, the winner 13 years earlier.

"That Don't Impress Me Much," and "You've Got a Way."
The radio singles, released together for the first time in North
America, had not been available on the original release.

Near the closing of her Thanksgiving night special,
Shania looked out at her fans and spoke to them. "Before
I say goodnight, there's a thought I'd like to leave you
with. If someone would have told me ten years ago I'd be
standing right here in front of all of you people tonight in
Dallas, Texas, I'd have told them they were out of their
minds. But maybe that's what dreams are all about. And
sometimes, they can even come true. That's a nice
thought to remember as we come to the end of any year,
let alone the end of a century."

By this time, Shania Twain's career was definitely
bigger than life.

Arriving at the 2000 Country Music Association Awards in Nashville, Shania waves to the crowd. Whatever the future holds for Shania, she can be sure that she has won her rightful place in country music.

8

WHAT DOES THE FUTURE HOLD?

SHANIA'S PLANS FOR the dawn of the third millennium included two albums to be released in 2000. To the disappointment of her many fans, those albums were put on hold.

She did, however, garner honors from BMI's Country Awards in October. Always wanting her songwriting talents recognized, Shania was delighted to be honored as Songwriter/Artist for "Come on Over," "That Don't Impress Me Much," and "Man! I Feel Like a Woman!"

Shania also announced that she would not tour in 2000, preferring to be out of the public eye for a while. She and Lange wanted time to write and produce their next album. When she appeared at the 2000 CMA Awards show, she talked backstage about their work. "At this stage," Shania explained, "we are really just being very creative. We're not giving the music any direction right now. We're just creating music. . . ." And she added: "Right now, we're still writing. And when you're writing, you're thinking concepts. . . you're thinking of lyrics.

You're not thinking about formats, style, really, and sound so much. So it's too early to tell what direction it's going to take."

As she has said before, "A lot of people think we have all these tricks up our sleeve. You know what? The trick is hits! If you have a hit song, then you have a career carpet to ride on. Without it, the carpet is just not gonna float."

Beyond that, her other plans remain more vague. She has dispelled speculation that she might write an auto-biography, citing her family's privacy as her rationale. "I'm not sure I ever will. I can't tell my story without revealing my family's, and I don't think that's really fair. My career has exposed them so much already. We're just so, I don't know if simple is the right word, but we're northern Ontario people, and I don't think we'll ever be accustomed to the Hollywood thing."

The Hollywood "thing" might imply film scripts, but Shania claims to be reluctant to make the leap to the silver screen. She feels she might not be any good at acting. Shania likes to be the best at what she does, and if she can't be, she's not interested.

The couple's plans are likely to change somewhat in the near future. They had thought about having children, and Shania had confessed in the past that she was considering it. But she had been ambivalent. According to her sister Carrie-Ann, Shania expressed a desire for children but changed her mind after a visit with Carrie-Ann and her children. Certainly Shania has had experience, even though she raised older children. And there is plenty of room in the sprawling estate in Switzerland she shares with Lange. The place is, as Shania has said, "a beautiful place to raise children."

At least one child will have the chance to find out. In March 2001, Shania and Lange proudly announced that a baby is on the way. According to the tabloid *National Enquirer*, Shania is "giddy with happiness." The paper rushed to quote a so-called insider who claimed that

This aerial view shows Le chateau de Sully, the sprawling estate in Switzerland that was built for a Swiss baron in 1882 and now serves as Shania and Mutt's home.

Shania had said: "I've always wanted to have a baby, but in my head, I always was thinking later rather than sooner. I guess later's finally arrived."

The newest Lange will enter a household with plenty of room for him or her, along with a large menagerie. Shania's dog, Tim, to whom she is so attached she has taken him on tour with her and who never strays far from her side, shares his life with cows, sheep, fowl, and five horses.

As for the couple's own lifestyle, they shun alcohol, and according to reports, they practice an East Indian form of meditation called Sant Mat. Both are also strict vegetari-

Shania always looks forward to time out of the public eye to enjoy private moments with her husband and her animals, including her dog, Tim. Her future plans, however, include a new baby to round out her contented family life.

ans. Lange had long been a vegetarian when he and Shania met, and his influence has kept her away from meat as well. Shania doesn't eat fish or eggs either, and she says she has much more energy because of her diet. But Shania does have a passion for pasta, her favorite food. She also says, "I eat a lot of tofu, and I drink soy shakes with fruit every morning. I always have soybeans, black beans, or chickpeas for lunch or dinner." It's no wonder she has been given the title of Sexiest Vegetarian Alive.

Only time will tell how much Shania will perform and record as she awaits the birth of her baby. With her drive and ambition, however, she will not likely fall far from the limelight. She has been nominated for three 2001 TNN/Country Weekly awards: Entertainer of the Year, Female Artist of the Year, and Impact Award. In fact, fans can vote on a Country Weekly website. The public can also have Shania's image with them all year long with a 2001 Shania calendar.

For the time being, however, Shania's focus will no doubt center on her husband and caring for a child. Family has always been a significant part of Shania's life, and she is not likely to allow her career to interfere with her closeness to those dear to her. But Shania will always move forward. As she once put it: "I've gone through some very dramatic stages in my life, and I feel three different people lived through those stages. It's funny, I often feel like I'm on my third lifetime." Perhaps she is looking forward to a fourth lifetime.

CHRONOLOGY

1965	Eileen Regina Edwards born to Clarence and Sharon Edwards on August 28 in Windsor, Ontario, Canada
1968	Parents separate; mother moves with three daughters to Timmins, Ontario
1971	Mother marries Jerry Twain, an Ojibwa Indian; Twain adopts the three girls, who become members of the Ojibwa tribe
1973	Begins singing and playing guitar in public at community gatherings
1978-1983	Plays and sings in clubs around Timmins and Sudbury, Ontario
1978	Meets country singer Mary Bailey, who will become mentor; appears on television on *The Tommy Hunter Show* in Toronto, Canada
1982	Makes unsuccessful trip to Nashville, Tennessee, to try recording
1983	Graduates from Timmins High and Vocational School
1984	Plays with band Longshot in Timmins area
1984-1987	Tours with bands in northern Ontario
1987	Leaves Timmins for Toronto; sings and plays in clubs in Toronto; opens show for Broadway musical star Bernadette Peters; parents killed in car crash; returns to Timmins
1988-1991	Moves with brothers and sister to Huntsville, Ontario; begins singing and performing in Deerhurst Resort
1991	Spotted by Nashville entertainment lawyer Dick Frank; signs contract with Mercury Nashville Records; moves to Nashville to record; changes name to Shania
1992	Records debut album, *Shania Twain*
1993	Debut album released; peaks at #68 on *Billboard*'s Top Country Albums chart; first and second singles, "What Made You Say That?" and "Dance with the One That Brought You," peak at #55 on *Billboard*'s Hot Country Singles chart; films video of "Dance with the One That Brought You"; meets British record producer Robert "Mutt" Lange; marries Lange on December 28
1994	Moves with Lange to Adirondack Mountains in New York State; begins recording second album, *The Woman in Me*
1995	Releases *The Woman in Me*; singles "Any Man of Mine" and "(If You're Not in It for Love) I'm Outta Here" hit #1 on *Billboard*'s Hot Country Singles chart; wins American Music Award for Favorite New Country Artist Performer

1996 Singles "You Win My Love" and "No One Needs to Know" hit #1 on *Billboard*'s Hot Country Singles chart; wins Academy of Country Music Award (ACMA) and Billboard Music Award for Country Album of the Year for *The Woman in Me* as well as Top New Female Vocalist Award from ACMA; with Lange wins Grammy Award for Best Country Album for *The Woman in Me*; newspapers reveal Jerry Twain is not her biological father; fires longtime manager Mary Bailey; signs with Landau Management

1997 Releases third album, *Come on Over*; sales of *The Woman in Me* reach 12 million worldwide

1998 Appears on VH-1 cable channel's *Divas Live* and on CBS special, "Shania Twain's Winter Break"; moves with Lange to home in Switzerland; begins North American concert tour

1999 Continues touring; performs for 20,000 fans in hometown of Timmins; appears in CBS television special, "Shania Twain: Come on Over"; wins Grammy Awards for Best Country Song for "You're Still the One" and for Best Female Country Vocal Performance; signs with Revlon as spokesperson; receives CMA Entertainer of the Year Award

2000 Voted one of Top Three Favorite Female Musical Performers by People's Choice Awards; wins ACMA Entertainer of the Year Award; American Music Awards Favorite Pop/Rock Female Performer; BMI Award for Pop Songwriter of the Year and Country Song Writer of the Year

2001 Pregnant with her first child; fourth album scheduled to be released

Glamorous and elegant, Shania performs at a Billboard *Music Awards gala. Her performance before a packed house in Las Vegas was a long way from the rowdy, smoky clubs of northern Ontario where she played her guitar and sang as a young girl.*

DISCOGRAPHY

Albums

1993   *Shania Twain*

1995   *The Woman in Me*

1997   *Come on Over*

Singles

1993   "What Made You Say That?"
            "Dance with the One That Brought You"
            "You Lay a Whole Lot of Love on Me"

1995   "Whose Bed Have Your Boots Been Under?"
            "Any Man of Mine"
            "The Woman in Me (Needs the Man in You)"
            "(If You're Not in It for Love) I'm Outta Here"

1996   "You Win My Love"
            "No one Needs to Know"
            "Home Ain't Where His Heart Is (Anymore)"
            "God Bless the Child"

1997   "Love Gets Me Every Time"
            "Don't Be Stupid (You Know I Love You)"
            "Come on Over"

1998   "You're Still the One"
            "From This Moment On"
            "Honey, I'm Home"
            "When"

1999   "That Don't Impress Me Much"
            "Man! I Feel Like a Woman!"
            "You've Got a Way"

2000   "Rock This Country"
            "Stuff That Matters"

Videos

1995   *Shania Twain*

1996   *The Complete Woman in Me*

AWARDS

1993   Rising Star Award from Country Music Television/Europe

1995   Favorite New Country Artist Performer from American Music Awards
(AMA); Album of the Year (*The Woman in Me*), Single of the Year ("Any
Man of Mine"), Female Vocalist of the Year from Canadian Country Music
Awards (CCMA)

1996   Top New Female Vocalist, Album of the Year (*The Woman in Me*) from
Academy of Country Music Awards (ACMA); Country Album of the Year
(*The Woman in Me*) from *Billboard* Music Awards (BMA); Female Vocalist
of the Year from CCMA; Favorite New Country Artist from Blockbuster
Entertainment Awards (BEA); Grammy Award (with Robert Lange) for
Best Country Album (*The Woman in Me*)

1997   Favorite Female Country Performer from AMA; Special Achievement Award
from CCMA

1998   Favorite Female Country Performer from AMA; Favorite Female Country
Artist; Favorite Single ("You're Still the One") from BEA; Female Vocalist of
the Year, Album of the Year (*Come on Over*); Single of the Year ("You're the
One") from CCMA

1999   Favorite Country Female Performer from AMA; Favorite Female Country
Artist, Favorite Single ("You're Still the One") from BEA; Female Vocalist of
the Year from CCMA; Grammy Awards for Best Country Song ("You're Still
the One") and Best Female Country Vocal; Entertainer of the Year from Country
Music Association (CMA)

2000   Entertainer of the Year from ACMA; Favorite Pop/Rock Female Performer,
Favorite Country Female Performer from AMA; Favorite Female Country Artist
from BEA; Pop Songwriter of the Year and Country Song Writer of the Year
from BMI

BIBLIOGRAPHY

Brown, Jim. *Shania Twain: Still the One*. New York: Quarry Press, 2000.

Gallagher, Jim. *Shania Twain*. Childs, MD: Mitchell Lane, 1999.

Gray, Scott. *On Her Way: The Shania Twain Story*. New York: Ballantine Books, 1998.

Hager, Barbara. *On Her Way: the Life and Music of Shania Twain*. New York: Berkley Boulevard Books, 1998.

Johns, Michael-Anne. *Shania Twain*. Kansas City, MO: Andrews McMeel, 1999.

Kane, Peter. *Shania Twain*. New York: Welcome Rain, 2000.

McCall, Michael. *Shania Twain: An Intimate Portrait of a Country Music Diva.* New York: St. Martin's Griffin, 1999.

Wendt, Tim. *Shania Twain*. New York: Apple Books, 1998.

INDEX

INDEX

PICTURE CREDITS

Dwayne E. Pickels is an award-winning reporter with the *Tribune-Review* newspaper in Greensburg, Pennsylvania. A magna cum laude graduate of the University of Pittsburgh, where he cofounded and edited the literary magazine *Pendulum*, Dwayne won a Pennsylvania Newspaper Publishers' Association Keystone Press Award in 1992. In 1997, Dwayne authored four volumes in the Chelsea House series Looking into the Past: People, Places and Customs. He also wrote a volume on psychological testing for Chelsea House. Dwayne currently resides in Scottdale, Pennsylvania, with his wife, Mary, and their daughter, Kaidia Leigh. In his free time, he is immersed in various literary pursuits—which include a novel based on Celtic myth and legend surrounding the ancient pagan festival of Samhain, the origin of Halloween. In addition to writing, Dwayne enjoys outdoor excursions, including bird watching, hiking, photography, cooking, and target shooting, along with typically futile attempts at fishing.

James Scott Brady serves on the board of trustees with the Center to Prevent Handgun Violence and is the vice chairman of the Brain Injury Foundation. Mr. Brady served as assistant to the President and White House press secretary under President Ronald Reagan. He was severely injured in an assassination attempt on the president, but remained the White House press secretary until the end of the administration. Since leaving the White House, Mr. Brady has lobbied for stronger gun laws. In November 1993, President Bill Clinton signed the Brady Bill, a national law requiring a waiting period on handgun purchases and a background check on buyers.